ON THE ROAD TO SAYING BYE TO

AUTISM

LAKISHA MARIE MACKIE

On the Road to Saying Bye to Autism
Copyright © 2023 Lakisha Marie Mackie

Because of the dynamic nature of the Internet, any web addresses or links contained in this book may have changed since publication and may no longer be valid. The views expressed in this work are solely those of the author and do not necessarily reflect the views of the publisher, and the publisher hereby disclaims any responsibility for them.

Library of Congress Control Number: 2022951179
Paperback: 978-1-958169-88-9
eBook: 978-1-958169-89-6

"Walking in the yard before school."

Always follow your dreams, never give up, keep pushing forward, and you will be happy and proud that you did.

—Lakisha Marie Mackie

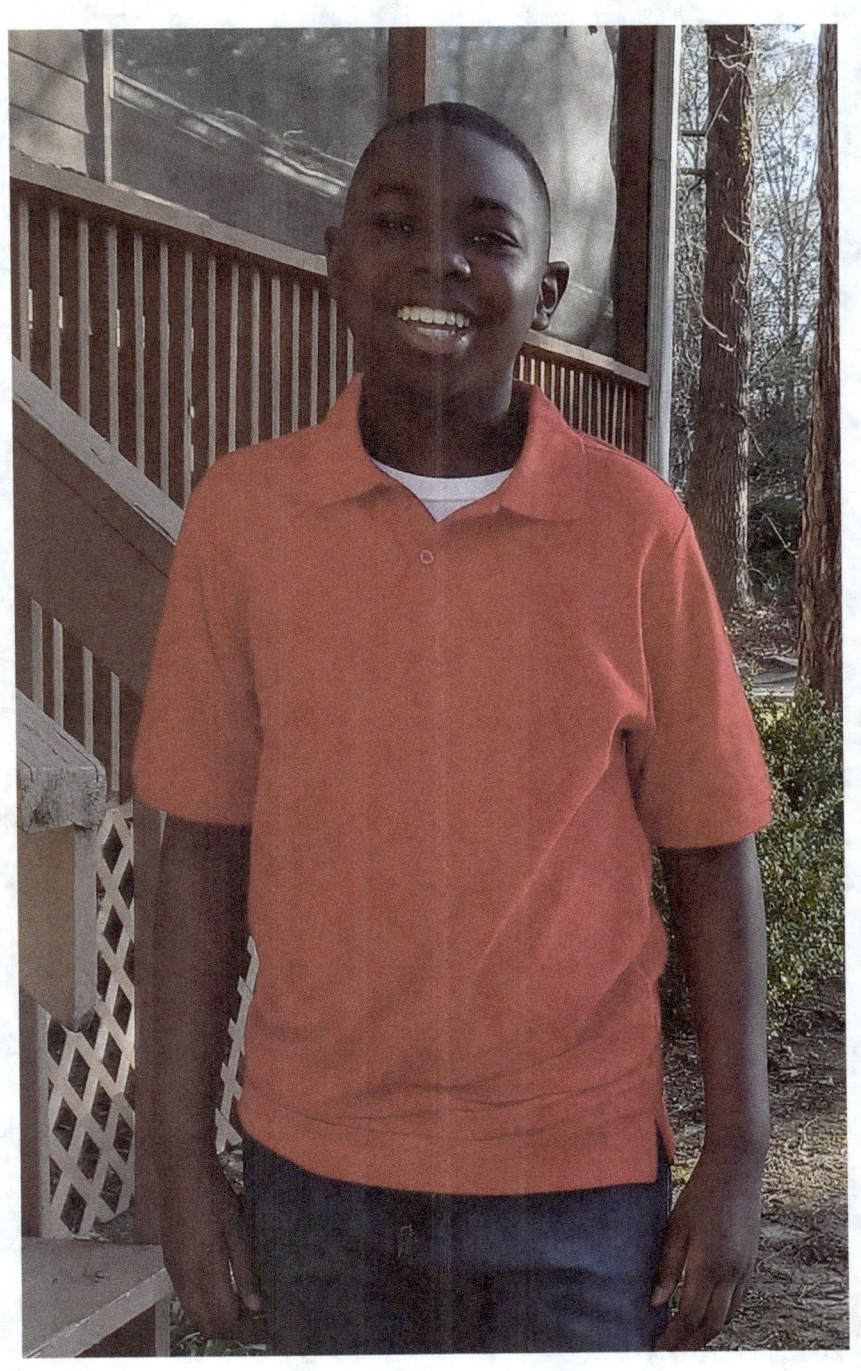

To LaDainian Mitchell McNeal, my loving son

Thinking about a pose for this picture.

I wrote this book to help other families out there who were having the same problems in their families. We all could use a little help. I wanted people to hear from a regular person who was having the type of problems I wrote about in this book. I am not a doctor. I'm not a herbalist. I'm just a regular person with a regular job who has a son with autism. This book is about all the things I did to help my son. I wrote about all the steps I took to get my son's brain on the right channel it was supposed to be on, and that was my goal, so I hope and pray that this book could help a lot of families, and if you don't want to do the research I did, then maybe this book will help you to start your own research. Thanks for taking the time to read my book.

Lakisha Marie Mackie

LaDainian Mitchell McNeal was born on December 22, 2009, at 8:47 a.m. at seven pounds fifteen ounces, twenty-one and a half inches long. I had gone home to visit. It was March or April. I used to try to go home to visit around the same time every year. My sister-in-law and one of my aunts were like, "Are you with child?" I was like, "What are y'all talking about?" My sister-in-law was like, "I know your breasts are big, but they are huge today." Mind you they haven't seen me in a long time. I am drinking beer, taking shots the whole nine yards. I got back here to Smyrna, Georgia, from Augusta, Georgia. And like a week later after being home from Augusta, Georgia, I started feeling so tired. I was working at Burger King as a shift manager, so I had to do all different shifts. One day I worked day shift I got off work at 5:00 pm I got home, lay on the couch and went to sleep. When I woke up, it was dark outside. I had my uniform on and all. I am saying to myself what the hell is wrong with me? My apartment was a mess. I was tired all the time, and sick. It never crossed my mind that yeah, I could be expecting. I looked at the calendar, and I said, "Man! It's only three or four days left in this month." I had gone to the store before then to get supplies because I kept feeling like my cycle was coming on cramping, sore breasts, tired, feeling fat. But nothing was happening them days had come and gone so fast. I got off work one day and went to the store and got a test out of the drugstore part of the store. The lady behind the counter was like, "I hope it works out the way you want it to." I said, "Right now I am feeling so sick." She said, "Well, get you some crackers." I said, "Okay." She said, "Yeah, that usually works." I bought some crackers too. I got home, took one of the tests, and it was three sticks in one box, and I took one test, and it said pregnant. I was like, "What!" No. So I took the other two, and they said pregnant. I was like, "Oh wow." I had all three sticks line up on my bathroom sink, just looking at all three of them. And I wanted a test to say not pregnant or pregnant, not no test with two lines or if it turns this color, no plain English. That's what I need.

So the first thing I thought about was man! All that drinking I was doing in Augusta, Georgia. I started to feel bad. "Is my baby okay?" That's what I needed to know. I was so worried. And drinking—that's not even me. Everybody was like, "You drinking a beer?" I was like, "I know right." So, I hurried up and looked online for a free clinic, and I found one and made an appointment. And the place I went to gives you three visits. Your first visit, of course they give you another test and ask you when your last cycle was and some other health questions, so after I took the test, the nurse said, "Yeah, you are pregnant, you are right at two months." I said, "Two months!" She said, "Yes, ma'am." I was like okay, and then she gave me some vitamins on my next visit. The third visit came, and I had a chance to see my baby for the first time. I was so happy that everything was okay. I was feeling sick all the time and tired. The last visit, they gave me a sonogram, and they gave me proof of pregnancy. I can take that letter to find a doctor or if I need government assistance, I can use that letter also. They can see that I am telling the truth. I had already told my mom that I was pregnant. She was like, "Yeah, I know." I called her that day too, and I said, "Well, I am two months, and the baby is doing great." She was like, "What!" I said, "Yeah, y'all was right." She said, "You already two months?" I said, "Yep." I took that letter to the best doctor in the world here in Smyrna, Georgia. I made an appointment.

They did the exam and took a bunch of blood. I asked the nurse, "Why do y'all have to do so many tubes of blood?" She said, "Not only can you be pregnant, but also you could have a STD." "Okay, thanks, nurse, that's what I want to hear." "Read more in First Book." They gave me a prescription for some vitamins and told me to drink a lot of water. "You are doing great, and we will see you next time." I was like, "Okay, so I am really having a baby." I was sick the whole nine months. I couldn't really eat nothing heavy. All I could eat were salads, grilled chicken, stuff like that. And I called the baby a boy the whole time. I said, "I know I'm having a boy, he giving me problems already when I went to the doctor the first time." They were like, "Are you sure you just two months?" I said, "Yes." They said, "You are showing like you are four months." They said, "Maybe it's twins." I said, "No, I already had my first sonogram, and it's just one baby." When they were examining me, that's when I found out that I had fibroids, and they seem to make you show bigger than you are. They also thought maybe I had the wrong due date. So after they found that out, I had to go to a specialist. They had to keep an eye on me because with those sometimes you can miscarry. The baby can have a hard time growing. I was already going to my lung doctor for my asthma. When I was carrying my son, I went to three different doctors—my OBGYN, my lung doctor, and the specialist.

My fibroids and my lungs were so bad off, the bigger I got, the harder it was for me to breathe. I couldn't wait to have my son. I always tell people it's not easy sharing your body with somebody that you don't know. I wanted him out so I could have my body back. I was sick all the time, couldn't eat what I wanted to eat. And when I would eat heavy like eating a big steak dinner. If I only ate a little of it, it felt like I had eaten my whole plate and somebody else plate too. And I was working the whole time. I maybe took off two days the whole nine-month period. I did bleed one time when I was pregnant. I guess I was working too hard. But I was not pouring blood. Once my manager found out I was expecting, they would give me three days off during the week instead of two days. So those three days I would stay in the bed, not moving. I would be on bed rest for three days out the week. I

On the Road to Saying Bye to Autism

put myself on bed rest. I would stay in bed, and not move unless I had to go to the restroom or get something to eat. Like I said in my first book, I was a shift manager; then I needed my rest. I think if I didn't put myself on bed rest, I might have had my baby early because one night I was having contractions, and I only was like seven months. I was doing too much. I was working, and then sometimes I had to walk to the bus stop to go home. But when I got to seven months, I started getting the cab home. I was getting too big to walk anywhere. Big old belly trying to walk, so they say. When you get close to time to have your baby, you start to clean up your nest. Nesting is what they call it.

I had got up this one morning, and my momma was here. She had come up to help me with the baby for a couple of weeks. She made breakfast. After I ate, I started mopping my dining room and kitchen floor. I was talking to my mom while I was mopping. I was standing there, and I was saying to myself, "I know I'm not standing here peeing on myself." I went to the bathroom, and I called my mom. Then I saw some clear stuff in my panties, and she was like, "Girl, your water broke." I said, "My water broke?" She said, "Yep, and we got to go to the hospital." I said, "But I'm not in no pain or nothing." I thought I was going to be like on TV: your water break, and you go right into having pain. Not me. I kept saying to my mama they were going to send me home. We had the radio in the car on and everything, still no pain. Before we got in the car, my mom was like, "Where is your bag, because we gone." I said, "My floor is not even done yet." I wanted to finish mopping my floor.

We got in front of the hospital doors, and I started to feel all this pressure. She said, "I told you." Now I got to the desk, and they asked my doctor's name, and I told them I was not registered or nothing. "All I have is this paperwork they gave me to take with me to the hospital." The nurse was doing that paperwork so fast, and I was still talking about "You don't have to rush. I am in no pain." She got the paperwork together and sent me upstairs and said she was going to let my doctor know I was at the hospital. So, I got upstairs, and they signed me in, in the triage room, and I put on this ugly gown. Then they take me to the delivery room. And I could have up to three people in that room, but I was crying because one person could be in the triage room. And I wanted my momma and my boyfriend in the room. Once I got out of that room, I walked down the hall to the next room. And I got them to call my Momma from downstairs, because I was in a regular room. They tried to put a IV in and couldn't. It took two or three people to get it. I said, "Well, I have not had anything to eat or drink since this afternoon." They couldn't find a vein. I wanted to tell the nurses off like I wasn't in enough pain, so once I got to the point where I could get the epidermal, my doctor came in and asked me if I want it. I was like yes. I was in so much pain. My momma said I went to sleep after that. I was so glad that pain was gone.

I only got to five centimeters, and the baby just stayed. He won't come down no more, so the doctor came in and said, "The baby's heart rate is dipping, and since you've been at five centimeters for so long, it would be best for the baby and you that we just do a C-section." I didn't care. I was tired, and I just wanted him out and healthy. I wanted him in his body and mine back. So, I went in December 21, 2009, in the afternoon. I had him on December 22, 2009, at 8:47 a.m. by C-section. And that was the day I was supposed to have him. He wasn't overdue, and I was so happy. I worked all the way up until I had him. My last day of work was December 18, 2009, and I had him on December 22, 2009. I couldn't afford to take off work, so they took him by C-section, and they said it's a boy. I heard him cry. I cried like a baby. I had gone through so much to have him and carry him. As soon as they got him cleaned up, and however long it takes for them to feed babies, they gave him a bottle. They said he was hungry. I was so mad they had given him a bottle because I had taken all these breastfeeding classes. They say babies can get confused between the bottle and the breast and might not want the breast. But thank God he did both—took the bottle and breastfed.

My mom was in my hospital room the whole time. She was great. She was rubbing my back when I was having labor pains. She had told the doctor or the nurse that she was a CNA, and them nurses hardly came in the room. They would come in there, but they weren't worried because they knew my mom could take care of me. They had her doing the baby intakes and out the whole time we were there. Every time the baby cried in the middle of the night, she got up to feed him. Because I really couldn't move, they made me get out that bed like the next day after my C-section. They were like, "Ms. Mackie, we need you to try and get out the bed to try and walk." And I was saying to myself, "Ok lady I did just have a C-section yesterday, and I gotta walk with this big smile in my stomach. Ok!! Really! So now it's time to go home. It was December 24, 2009. They were letting everybody who was well and able go home to spend Christmas at home. Man! I was happy. I was happy to go home to be in my own bed, and my mom was too. She was so tired.

The nurse had told me before I left the hospital not to have sex before six weeks. She said, "I know you had a C-section, but you still gotta wait six weeks. Don't go home lifting anything heavy or doing any heavy housework. Don't even lift your baby." They didn't want me to tear anything and have to come back to the hospital. I lift that baby every night. I wasn't going to get my mama up every time he cried. She did that in the hospital. She needed her rest. I wanted to take care of my own baby. But she helped during the day if I wanted to take a nap or a shower. She took care of the baby while I did that. She left a couple days after I got home. She had to get back to work, but she was coming back to stay for good in March of 2010 because I was supposed to go back to work in March, and since I was so scared of day care, I was going to pay her to keep my baby during the day while I worked. I didn't want her to leave. My son had started having stomach problems. That milk they were giving him in the hospital didn't agree with him. So he ended up having colic (gas), and he had got a rash on his face. He had an allergic reaction to the milk. So it gave him colic, and gave him a rash in his face. So he cried for 3 or 4 months straight. Every day same time. Every day 5:00 p.m. until whenever I was walking the hallway with him, trying to get him to burp or pass gas or something, so he finally got over that. It took a while because I had to get him a different kind of milk. Since in the hospital, he had gotten so used to drinking milk out of a bottle my milk wasn't coming in fast enough for him, so he would breastfeed some and bottle-feed some. The plan was to breastfeed only, but the hospital messed that up.

So he turned one year old. And he did everything early. He was walking before one year old, crawling, rolling over, and cutting teeth. He did all that early. I was saying to myself, "Okay, by the time he turn two years old, that speech is going to start coming too. We were talking to him, reading to him everything." But I noticed when he was one or one and a half year old, he would spin fast, just spinning all day long, and he would never seem dizzy. He would always have to have something in his hand, and always had things in his mouth that wasn't made to eat. He was doing some things I had never seen a kid do before. So one day, I had a WIC office appointment. They give you free food and milk for your child. Read more in the first book *The Truth You Didn't Know*. The lady asked me if I had any concerns about his health or anything. So I was like yes, his speech. I said, "He is not saying momma or daddy or nothing." So she gave me the name of this program that help kids with speech. She said, "I can have them call you." I was like "Yes, please." He was two years old by this time, and they called. I set up an appointment, and they told me the first thing that had to go was that thumb. I said, "Yeah, he found his thumb at three months old and haven't let go since." They said, "Yes, that has to go." He said, "Second, he needs to be around other kids and adults besides y'all. Y'all been here ten or fifteen minutes, and he is not trying to play with her or with her toys. He been hanging on to you the whole time."

There was this guy talking to me, and there was a lady in there too. She was trying to get him to play with her while we talked. I took in all that information, and when I got home, me and my momma got him off that thumb sucking. It took about three weeks. It was like he was having withdrawals. He cried all night. We had it all wrapped up. He would only suck the right thumb. Sucking the other one didn't feel right. I didn't have to worry about him going to the other thumb. Then the other advice he gave me was he needs to be around other adults and other kids. That sound like day care to me, so the program he was in would come to the daycare he was at and have speech therapy with him. As it was a few other kids who was in the same program he was in. That had to have speech therapy too. He had like a two in one deal. Everybody kept telling me he was going to start getting sick all the time now, and I was like, "Why does everybody keep saying that?" But it was because he was going to be around all those new germs. He was only around family, mostly adults and no kids. He wasn't around kids at all. He is the only child, he has no brothers or sisters yet.

He got in day care, and it took him about two or three weeks to get used to being there. He cried every time he got dropped off. He wasn't used to people outside of family. I blame myself for that, but he got used to being there, but the eating part. He wouldn't eat what they had there. He didn't like the food. He is such a picky eater. He only wants the same thing every day—nuggets, fries, pizza, peanut butter and jelly. That's why when he saw that lady in his room at day care and she had that fry box, he wanted some. She would buy him a fry every day so he would have some type of food in his system. I would forever be grateful for that. Read more in first book "The Truth You Didn't Know". Sure enough, he did get sick all the time— ear infections, runny nose, coughing, the whole nine yards. He never had none of those things until then. We stayed at the ER or his doctor because he'd be sick with different germs, and when one of us got sick, we made sure we stayed out of his face. At day care, this kid sick, then he touched your kid now your kid is sick. I also noticed how he never really wanted to play with the kids. He would always be by himself, so I just guessed, "Well, he is used to being by himself." Then he would never come when we called his name. I would say, "Well, maybe he can't hear." Then I noticed how he would line up his cars and look at them. He would look at himself in the mirror for long periods of time, and at day care, if it was somebody's birthday party, they would tell me, "Oh, he didn't eat his cupcake or cake or ice cream." I would tell them that was okay, I never gave him sweets, he was already full of energy. He didn't need anything extra. The program he was in for speech had told me what school he would be going to for his pre-K. It was a regular school with Special Education classes.

When he started day care, he was like two or two and a half years old. He couldn't start pre-K until he was three years old, so he stayed in day care until then. Day care was where he learned some structure

On the Road to Saying Bye to Autism

because at home all he did was run around all day long, spinning around in circles. He wouldn't sit long enough for me to read him a story or try to teach him his ABCs. He couldn't sit long enough at home. He didn't have a certain time for nap or lunch. In school or day care, you get a time for this and that, and he had to learn when it was time to sit and listen and a time to play. He went from not eating to eating what they had, not playing with the kids to trying to play with them. This was when he was in day care. He was doing so good from the time when we first started him in day care. It took some weeks, but he got used to it. And I felt bad at first, because I was like, "Man! I threw my son in the lion's den." He didn't understand why he was there and why we were leaving him. But when he started pre-K, the first day of school, me and his dad took him, and he just went inside the classroom, and sat down no crying or nothing, 3 years old now!

I was shocked. I felt like crying. my son is growing up. He had come a long way since those first weeks in day care. Before he started pre-K, we all had a meeting, and I had to answer a couple of pages of questions like, does he or she come when you call his or her name? Does he or she spin in circles? Questions like those. Even in the program he was in, the same kind of questions. It seems like you never stop answering questions. But the meeting was about the goals they were setting for my son as far as his speech and other therapy that he would have during the day while he was in school. I started to cry, because I started feeling really bad, and I asked them, was it anything that I had done wrong? Was it something else I should have been doing while he was younger? They said, "It was nothing you did wrong, but he is in the right place now. Sometimes things just happen."

I blamed myself. I still blame myself. When I was carrying my son, sometimes I listened to classical music. They said that helps with your baby's brain development, so I did that. I listened to it with him, some nights even after I had him. One time I put on Janet Jackson. He loves music. He always has. It just can't be too loud. I also noticed how he cover his ears with his hands when loud music was on and loud noise. If people are talking too loud, he will cover his ears. Now they told me in the meeting that he needed to take a hearing test before he could start pre-K. They asked me, at birth did he pass his hearing test? And I told them yes. They said, "We just want to make sure he can hear." I said, "Yes, he passed at birth, but sometimes he acts like he doesn't hear me when I call his name."

My son watched *Sesame Street* and all those other shows that come on that GPB channel I used to prop him up. He was like three or four months, and I let him watch *Sesame Street* Cookie Monster, and listen to them count and say their ABCs, and he would watch it. He liked the songs they sing, and this was at the same time he was going through that colic stage, but he was a perfect baby up until 5:00 p.m. every day when he was crying, and I was walking with him down the hall all night. I would sing to him his ABCs and counting and talking to him and telling him he was going to be okay. That's why I couldn't understand, like why my kid? I did the classical music, I read to him, I talked to him, sing to him—everything. I breastfed him up to six months old. They said breast milk helps brain development in babies. I didn't want my son going through what I went through in school. Read more in first book "*The Truth You Didn't Know*." So yeah, I was going to start teaching my son things like counting and his ABCs early.

Thank God he was able to start school early. He started school at three years old for pre-K. He passed his hearing test. I answered all the questions they asked me to answer, and they started him out with sign language. That helped out so much because what he would do was pull me to the kitchen, and I have to stand there and figure out what he wanted. The program he was in said he is not supposed to be pulling you anywhere. He is supposed to tell you what he wants. With the sign language, he could sign drink, or cup, or milk, or more milk. His teacher said he picked up on that fast. I was so happy. That was like a load off me, and then came a few words. He was doing good. The speech therapist would tell us to make him say what he wants. When he is at home with y'all. If he doesn't say it, then he doesn't get it.

I made it my goal to find out what I can feed him or what kind of vitamins I can give him every day to help him speak. What made me decide that was him not wanting to eat different foods. If he never ate it before, then he doesn't want it, without even knowing how it might taste. All he wanted to eat every day were nuggets, cheeseburgers, fries, pizza, peanut butter and jelly sandwiches, grilled cheese sandwiches, and snacks—same things every day. I started running out of things to feed him and ideas or tricks to use to get him to eat different foods. I had started my own research reading books, and things like that. I wanted the spinning to stop. I can deal with him being full of energy, but I can't deal with him after he eats, then he wants to get from the table and run and jump around. I can't deal with that. And we ask him to sit down, and he starts crying me having to answer for him when we are out. Those things gone or not so much of I would be very happy. He just spins a little now not much anymore, and I would love for him when I ask him "LaDainian, how was school today?" and he'd be able to say school was good. But he is a very smart kid. When we are in the car and he is going to the doctor, he knows his way. He would be in the backseat with his head down and about to cry. He hates going to the doctor. He knows his way there, to family homes, to the dentist. Real smart.

Then he started pre-K. The teacher didn't know if he would be able to understand what they would be doing in class, but the first day of school, she said, "Oh yeah, he understands very well." I never said he was a dumb kid, and never will. That's my child. I would give him both my arms if he needed them. When he was younger, when he first started walking, he would tear up everything, toys everywhere, just getting into everything like most kids do. He had a nickname, little DOC. It went from little DOC to Hurricane quick. A family member gave him the nickname little Doc. But once he started walking, it went from little Doc to Hurricane fast. Because he will tear up a room. He was getting into everything. His nickname been Hurricane ever since. He just don't like to see things neat and clean. His room is always a mess.

My goal was to research every fruit and vegetable. I wanted to know what fruit and vegetable did what. What do carrots do? What do spinach do? If I had to stay up all night on the computer looking for answers, that's what I would do. My plan was to make him different juices in my blender, and juice him the fruits and vegetables that he is supposed to have on a daily basis. If he was not going to eat his fruit and vegetables, then he was going to drink them. I had been giving him vitamins since he was two years old. I did everything I was supposed to do, so before he started pre-K, me, his dad, and LaDainian had a meeting at his new school with two ladies that were head of the special education department I guess, and I had to answer more questions. Then the ladies would which places. The one that was playing with my son would come talk to us. They would take turns. This was the first meeting. I had asked them both, "Did I do anything wrong?" They said it was nothing that I did, that he is in the right place, and I felt a little better after that.

On the Road to Saying Bye to Autism

You don't want your kids to have any type of problems, none, and I blame myself for a lot of things. Did I work too much while carrying him? Did I not read to him enough? They really don't even know how you get autism. Some people say it could come from the genes. Some people say it comes from immunization shots. They really don't know. So, at this point, I was like, "You know what? I want to know how to get rid of it." That was the question I had in my head at that point. I didn't care how he got it. How do I get rid of it? I don't like to give my son medicine. I never have, so when I decided to do my own research, I knew it would be the natural way. Some people go the medicine route I am going the natural route, and I been taking vitamins since I was a kid myself. I kept a journal, and you can see in the back of the book what I did to help my son heal his brain, almost like a report.

Most of these vitamins give you energy, like the B12, so I wanted to make sure that he took his vitamins in the daytime while he was at school so he could burn some of the energy off. He was already a fun ball of energy before these new vitamins. I didn't write in the journal every day, but I tried to write in it at least every other day. I wanted to keep a track of everything that was going on. I moved to Smyrna, GA, September 3, 2005. I worked two jobs, went from zero jobs to two jobs. Read more about it in my first book (*The Truth You Didn't Know*), so I was working at this one restaurant as a cook/cashier, and then they had to close down because they weren't making enough money. I had gone on a cruise, and when I got back, I had to find me a job because I didn't have one, so I started working at Burger King. So I got a call to come in for an interview at the same spot that had closed down. Somebody had bought the building and turned it into something else. The new people that bought the place said they wanted me to work for them, me and a couple of people they liked, but they were changing the inside up, and it wasn't going to be open until like a month or so. I needed a job before then. I got a job at Burger King, which was right across the street from this restaurant. I promised the manager at Burger King that I wouldn't leave. She said "Okay, well, come do the interview anyway," and I did, and I got hired. They had already wanted us, and we had already done our application, so I guess maybe couple weeks, they started hiring more people.

One of my friends who was working there too was trying to hook me up with this guy that was new. They had gone to school together. She told me he was a good guy. "I never heard him being in any trouble or nothing," she said. "Go on ahead and give him your number." She had to tell me a few times "To give him my number." I said, "Okay, I trust you." So, I did. One day, he gave me a ride home from work. I just stayed down the street, and I gave him my number and I told him to use it sometimes, and he said, "OK, but I didn't think he would call." I said to myself, "He is not going to call. What took me so long to give him my number was because to me he looked like he stayed in trouble, but like he used to tell me, "I just look like this." We didn't really start talking on the phone and going out until December 2006.

I started working at that job probably in October 2006 because there were a lot of different things the owners wanted to do with the restaurant. He didn't work at this restaurant before it got bought out, so he didn't start there until later on. He called me, and we talked on the phone for a while. We had a lot in common. He was born in New York. I was born in New York. He has family in Augusta, Georgia, and I am from Augusta, Georgia. He started naming schools in Augusta, Georgia. I told him, "You don't know nothing about Augusta, Georgia." He said, "I would go down there every summer." I said to myself, "Okay, this might work." That first conversation on the phone was good. I didn't think we would hit it off like that. He was nothing how he looked. One time he took me home to Augusta, GA, to visit my family. We had been talking for a while by this time, and he asked me, "What if they don't like me?" I told him, "I'm not taking you home for nobody's approval. I am taking you home so they can meet you." I didn't care if they didn't like him or not. I liked him. I wasn't gonna change my mind about him if they didn't like him, but we got there, and everybody liked him. He stayed with his family, and I stayed with mine but let everybody tell it we were staying together, as soon as we met, and that wasn't the case. Yeah, he would spend the night, but he didn't move in with me until I had to go into the hospital in 2007. I woke up and couldn't breathe. Read more in the first book (*The Truth You Didn't Know*). I really thought that was the end for me, and I was scared to stay by myself. After that, people at work, even thought we were staying together before I got sick. And it wasn't like we sat down and talked about moving in together. "Oh, you going to move in at this time?" "Nope, it just happen. And I was so happy, because like I said, I was scared to stay by myself."

I guess he felt the same way I did. When we had our son, he was with me at the hospital. The triage room could only have one person in the room. I wanted my boyfriend in the room with me and my momma. My mom had come all the way from Augusta, Georgia, and it wouldn't be fair for her to sit in the lobby, so he was like, "You want me to leave and get your mama?" I said, "No, I want both of y'all in here." That's when the nurse told me, "This is just the triage room. You can have up to three people in your delivery room." I said okay, because my momma came from out of town. I got in the delivery room, and he went and got my momma from the lobby. They both were in the room. Then he was like, "I got to eat something." My mom stayed in the room until the doctor told me I had to have a

C-section. Then he came back to the room, and my mom asked him if he was going to be okay in there. And he said, "Yeah, I'm good." She told us, "I will see y'all when y'all get back."

He did good. I thought he was going to pass out. December 2016 will be ten years since we've been together. He was the first person to hold his son, and then he brought him over to me, and I was only able to tell him hey and kiss him on his cheek. With the C-section and all you can't move. We had our ups and downs, especially after the baby was born. I couldn't get my job back, so all the bills were on him. We both had a lot on our plate back then, but we made it through. When my son started day care, he was able to get on a schedule, before then he went to bed whatever time he wanted to, no kind of structure. I would have to be at work at 6:00 a.m. He would still be up playing at eleven o'clock. Twelve o'clock at night and I'm sitting in a chair in the living room tired as hell. All because I didn't want to hear him cry because he didn't want to go to sleep.

He started day care. I had to be at work at 6:00 a.m. The day care opened at 6:00 a.m., so his dad would drop him off. He would be the first one there sometimes. He went from six to two. Everybody kept telling us once he start day care, he was going to start getting sick all the time, and he did—infections, fever. When he got sick like that, I would keep him at home, he wasn't used to all those different germs. He was just used to being around me and his dad and his grandparents. One time he got sick, and I was too scared to call in at my job because I had already called once that week, and the day he got sick was payday. I knew they were going to give me a hard time for calling in. That's how some fast food jobs are. You can't get sick or anybody in your family. They just want you to show up at their stupid job, making $7.25 an hour. Me with my dumbass, I let him go on to day care that day. I was crying walking into my job because he was sick, and I wanted to be with him, not at my job. As soon as I left from work I took him straight to the hospital. After that day, I promised myself never to put any job before my son. I felt so bad that day I could hardly work. I thought about him all day.

His schedule was getting up at five or five thirty every morning. His bedtime was 7:30 p.m. Lights was out at my house no later than 8:30 p.m. It was no longer still up at eleven o'clock, twelve o'clock at night. Till this day lights out by 8:30 p.m. The only way he is up past 8:30 p.m. is if it's Friday, or I am running behind with dinner or whatever. Everybody around here is in bed by 9:30 p.m. or sitting watching TV or reading quietly. When he started day care, he had to learn when it's time to play, and when it's time to sit and listen. That's why the first day of school in pre-K he just went on in the classroom and sat down. I almost cried nothing like how he was in day care the first two or three weeks he just went on in the classroom like he had been doing that for years. His first day of school me and his dad took him. That second day of school he went on the school bus. No actually it was a couple of weeks. But he got on that bus like a sport. He loves riding the bus to this day. Three years old now riding the bus!! The little bus. He got on that bus like he been doing it for years. He had loved the school bus ever since.

They have two people on those buses—the bus driver and the monitor. I love that one summer he had to go to ESY (Extended School Year) because they wanted him to have extra help over the summer, and they didn't want him to forget anything that he had learned during the school year. ESY is for students who wasn't doing too well during the school year and needed extra help during the summer break; plus, they wanted to see if he would be able to adjust to a different school and teacher (during the summer) because he went to the same school, same teacher from three years old to five years old. That is a long time to be with one teacher all those years, and he was very attached. He didn't want to get off the bus if he didn't see her standing there waiting on the bus. She had him from a baby just like me.

He did great in ESY. His pre-K teacher was at the same school where he was at. He would see her, but she was in another class. She called me the first day of school and said his new teacher told her he did awesome the first day of school. I was so happy. They weren't sure if he would be able to adjust to all the new changes, but he did, and all this was before all the extra vitamins he was taking. I had asked his kindergarten teacher if he needed ESY this summer 2016, and she said no. She said he was doing so well he didn't need ESY. I was like "Okay, great, "but then I thought about it, and it wouldn't be good if he had to go because ESY was for students who needed extra help. That wasn't doing good during the school year. That means he was not understanding and not meeting his IEP goals for the school year and he needed extra help during the summer break. You want your kid to learn and grow and not need ESY. That means he is understanding; he is learning. The summer before he needed ESY but not for the summer of 2016. I was proud.

I know this is getting off the subject, but I was watching this show, and the lady said she doesn't like when men are at a woman's baby shower, that they should have their own. Not at my baby shower, I had guys there, and we had a good time. We didn't play no games. We just listened to music, ate very well, and it was just like a big party. I didn't want no finger food. I wanted some real food. Read more in first book, "*The Truth You Didn't Know*." I just had to say that I see nothing wrong with guys being at baby showers.

They had been testing LaDainian off and on all those years when he was at the first school I would have to answer pages and pages of questions, but I didn't mind him being tested or answering the questions. Because I knew all it was gonna do was help him. They would say sorry for all the questions. I would say no, it's not a problem because I knew it was only going to help him. It was only going to help him to talk and be on the level he needs to be on. The earlier the better. They told us when he was four years old that he had autism. When I got that news, when I read it on that paper, I cried, and I felt really bad, but I said, "Okay, now we know, let's fix it, let's face it now." I felt bad because like I said earlier in this book I did everything I was supposed to do. I read to him, I talked to him, I sang to him, breastfed him the first six months of his life. I listened to classical music. Breastmilk is supposed to help with brain development, so why didn't it work for my child? Really, autism! I did everything you are supposed to do, and my child ended up with autism. What the hell, man! His dad was so upset. He couldn't even go to work that day. I found out the results in the mail, so I went to the mailbox, read it, and I was like "Aaah s—."

I had heard of kids having autism, but I didn't know what it was, so I told his dad, I said, "You remember the last time they tested boo." I call him boo most of the time. He said yes. I said, "Well, they said he got autism." He was like you bullshitting. I said nope, and I showed him the letter. He read it while he was getting ready for work. He worked at night. He didn't go that night. That was a rough day. I blame myself. As a parent, you want your child to be healthy and strong with no problems. This world is so evil, but I was so glad that he was able to start school early with his birthday being so late. I was giving LaDainian the extra vitamins, but I would never stop his speech therapy or any other services he got during a school day. I wrote this book to help other families, so they can see what or can read what I did to help my son. I didn't want to give my son medicine. I hated giving him medicine when he was sick. He is a very smart kid. When he would get sick, and we are in the car taking him to his doctor. He knows his way. He knows his way to the doctor, and to his grandparents' house, and to school when we would be on our way to take him to the doctor. He be in the backseat with his head down, and hands over his ears. Because he knows his way. He didn't like going to the doctor. What kid do?

He had come a long way from when he was in day care the first couple of weeks. I thought my son would hate me for life for putting him in day care, but he got over it. My son did everything early. He walked early, crawled early. Teeth came in early. I just knew he would talk early since everything else he had done was early, but I see talking was taking a little longer, but I was going to make sure I did all I could to help him talk. If it took all my money to do so. I got tired of answering for him when people would ask him questions like "How are you doing? You have fun in school?" There was something in his brain that wasn't turned on, like a part of his brain wasn't on the right channel. I needed to find out how to get that part of his brain on the right channel and I believe that these new vitamins that he was on could help with that. I believe that the new vitamins and at least two juices I came up with would help him out a whole lot. All of us would drink the juices that he got on the weekends. He only got the juice on the weekends, since he had the vitamins during the week. The juices were like dessert for us for the weekend, a nice treat.

During the summer of 2016, since he was out of school for two months, I put the vitamins in his PediaSure, all of them except for the fish oil. He had all day to drink that PediaSure. It was going to take all day for him to do that. I believe and prayed so hard that these vitamins and juice would help him. I prayed that between the vitamins and the juices he wouldn't have a choice but to talk. I prayed that the vitamins or the juice would turn that channel on in his brain. Everybody thought he had gained weight with the vitamins. He really gained weight with the juices. I wanted to write this book to help other people out there who want to go the natural way in healing their kids. I do believe that all families will be able to say bye to autism. All families who are having these same issues can say "Bye," to autism.

LaDainian takes great pictures now. When he was in day care, they tried to get him to take pictures. He would try to get off the little stage they had. They even had one of the teachers sit with him, and they had it where you could not see the teacher, but he still didn't want to sit and take the pictures. We would take plenty of pictures of him at home, but these were professional pictures, and he wasn't used to that. And if it was one of the kids in day care birthday the parents would bring cake or cupcakes. They would say LaDainian didn't eat his cake. They would tell us he didn't eat his cake or cupcake or cookies whatever they would have. I would say, "Oh, that's OK." I don't give him cake and cookies. I wasn't giving him any sweets at all. He already was full of energy And I didn't want to add to that. He didn't start eating stuff like that until he was like 4 or 5 years old. He is a very smart kid, and if he was being bad at home, all I had to do was tell him to sit down or go to his room. Boy you tell him to do those things you just messed up his whole world. He always was moving, couldn't sit still. Telling him to sit down and be quiet, that was punishment for him.

I knew something had to change with his diet. I knew he needed more fruits and vegetables in his diet. He needed more than just the vitamins and the PediaSure. He needed more than that for that channel to turn on in his brain. That's why I came up with the two juices. I knew he couldn't eat nuggets and fries, and pizza all his life, so if he wasn't going to eat his fruits and vegetables, then he was going to drink them. I did a lot of praying and a lot of thinking of ways to get him to eat his vegetables and fruits. When he was an infant, he ate fruits and vegetables all the time, so it's not like he never had them. I couldn't understand that part.

I did research on the fruits and vegetables he is supposed to have because I wanted to know what was in these fruits and vegetables. You can see the research in the back of this book. Like I said before, if I have to look up every fruit and vegetable, that's what I was gonna do. What do spinach do? What do squash do? I didn't have to go online. Thank God most of my research came from my health books that I already had. I read one book on autism, and I had planned on getting some more just to see what other people did. I felt what I was doing was right. When LaDainian was like two years old, he was getting his hair cut. And just crying, and I was sitting in the chair with him, he was sitting on my lap. He was crying, and having a fit, because at this time or age he hated getting his hair cut. So he just up and said, "I want my momma." I said Boo I am sitting right here. Me and his Dad looked at each other, and was like, "did you hear that?" That was the first time he said a full sentence. He said I want my momma while he was crying. I was in shock. He was two-years old then. We had not heard him say a full sentence since. And we both wanted to hear that again. I mean he do now sometimes. He is 7 years old now so sometimes he will say a full sentence. At 2, he was able to talk. We just had to figure out how to get his brain on the right channel. Getting him help early helped too. And we took advice from people who was helping us. Like his teacher, and his therapists. The research on the fruits and vegetables, and vitamins—that was just extra help along with his therapy that he was getting in school. Along with a lot of praying and thinking. My goal was to get his brain on the right channel.

I did think of ways to get my son to eat. What could I do? People would tell me. If I wouldn't make him extra to eat besides what we were eating. He would get hungry enough to eat what I had cooked. I would never do that. I make his plate with what we are having, and it would just sit there, and yes, I would make him something different to eat. You can roll your eyes at me, not like me, call me whatever name you want, but I'm not sending my child to bed hungry. He would lose weight, and then the police would be knocking on my door asking me questions. Nope. I would just rather make him something, and I really don't believe those same people would do the same. Do their kids like that? They wouldn't send their kids to bed without eating. But telling me to do my son like that. I am not doing it. LaDainian would give me his cup when he wanted something to drink. And he would run off. When he was using the toddler cup or even with his regular cup. I stop filling the cup up, and I tell him you gotta tell me what you want, milk? Or juice? And if he didn't tell me I would put the cup back down. He would give me the cup and run off to go play. Sometimes, he would say. Sometimes, I would have to give him a choice and make him say. Like the man was telling us in the program he was in, he is not supposed to be pulling you anywhere he is supposed to tell you what he wants, when he pulls me in the kitchen. I gotta stand and figure out what he wants. He would pull us to the door too. If he wanted to go outside to play them was some rough times.

LaDainian had graduated from kindergarten on May 23, 2016, and I was fighting tears. Then he got a reward for most improved in reading. I was so happy. I didn't know about that. That was a surprise for me and his dad. I was saying to myself, "Go LaDainian." I was so proud, and his dad was too, so I figured we should take him to his favorite spot, IHOP, for pancakes. He loves IHOP. Then we took him back to his old school where he did Pre-K. That school is home for us. We always take pictures to the teachers. He gets to see everybody, and I am always happy we took LaDainian back to his old school. One of the teachers there that knew him said, "I'm claiming him in my class for fifth grade." I said, "the school he is at now got him for first grade, but he will be back here for second grade for sure." It's so many kids with disabilities. They can't put everybody at the same school. So the school he went to pre-K at was his home school. When one day he doesn't have autism no more he can always go back to his home school. If we are living in that school area, that is truly our family. I said, "They got him for the first grade, but I am claming him back here for second grade." And the teacher I was talking to said, "Yeah, I hear you." They love my son. That is truly our family. My plan was to give my son a party when he started talking, and all were invited because we all were waiting on that. We all wanted him to do well and succeed. May 25, 2016, was a month since he had been taking the B12 and the fish oil. He was doing so well taking those vitamins at that point. Half the time he didn't even want anything to drink after he took the vitamins. In the beginning he needed juice or something to drink after it. I did all that worrying for nothing. He was sleeping longer and longer in his bed at night. I pray for the day when he will sleep in his bed all night.

LaDainian had gone out of town with his grandparents in May 2016 to Florida. Whenever he can go and get away from here, I'll let him. He needs to be around other people besides his parents. They had gone to visit family there on his dad's side. It helps him a lot to be around kids his age and other adults besides me all the time, and he had day care and school helped him out a lot when it came to him being around other people beside us. Adults and other kids, he wasn't used to people outside of family. And like I said before, I blame myself for that. I have until 2018 to get LaDainian brain on the right channel. It was supposed to be on. By that time, he will be ready for second grade and back at his old school. I made that my number one goal. And I believe if I kept on doing what I was doing. He was going to get to that point where he is talking your ears off. The summer of 2016 we had our summer school at home. Monday through Friday he was taking vitamins, and juice on the weekends. Saturday and Sunday was family time, especially on Sundays, because me and his dad didn't have to work on Sundays. The weekend was family time and juice drinking chill time. I had to get LaDainian ready for first grade, so school work was just writing his name, and his letters, numbers and coloring. Plus, the kindergarten teacher had given him a summer school packet with a lot of worksheets, so we did it. At night before he went to bed, I read him a bedtime story. He'd always liked that. I did not want him to forget any of what he had learn during the school year, over the summer break, and after a while he got used to me saying, "Come on, boo, you got homework to do." He would come to where I was in the living room and sit down and do his homework. Well, whatever I had planned for us to do.

Now don't get me wrong. I didn't just give him his vitamins, and he woke up one day and started talking and doing what other kids did. But I did start to see improvements within a month's time. It took time because I was going the natural way. These vitamins and juices were working for him along with prayer, and a whole lot of thinking. This is not medicine, so it's gonna take time. It's not gonna happen overnight. I wish it did. But every day, I felt like I was on the right track. He was saying more and more words. And the words were becoming clearer. You could understand him, and he was trying to put those words together. I kept praying every day and thinking now they say early prevention is best. And it is. When I started talking to people about his speech delay, he was two years old. When we went to the WIC office, and I told that lady he wasn't talking. He was 2 years old or 2 ½ years old. He wasn't 3 yet.

He was either two or two and a half years old, and he's been in school since he was three years old, so he's been going to speech therapy and been tested at a very early age. Now he is trying to say more words and make a sentence. And I got him this juice and these vitamins to move him right along a little faster. The earlier the better is the best way to go. The earlier the better is the best way to go if you think anything is wrong, start asking questions, like he wasn't talking, and I didn't know why and I wanted to know why. I'm glad I opened my mouth and told that lady I had concerns about his speech. I said, "He is not saying anything." Everybody could see that he was improving—his grandparents, his dad. And like I said, that was like in a month's time. You can see in the back of this book a record that I kept on his progress.

If your kid is older than six years old and you're just now getting help for your kid and doing research like I did, it's never too late. I saw one kid, well, a grown man who had autism going off to college! So, there is hope, it is something that can be fixed. You can heal from it. That was proof right there, and that was all I needed to see. I was happy for the young man. The best advice I can give is do your own research. Find what's best for you and your family. If you read this book and you feel in your gut that this research is not the truth or false, then go do what you feel is right. I feel in my gut that what I was doing to help my son was right for him, and it seemed to be working for him. Everybody in the family saw how he was improving. Like I said earlier, I wrote this book to help other families who were going through the same things. I felt like these vitamins and juice were going to turn my son's brain on the right channel it was supposed to be on. That part of his brain was off, and these vitamins and juice was gonna turn it on. I felt in my gut that what I was doing was the right thing. Just like when I was carrying him. I went to a specialist for my fibroids. And she said, "would you like to know what you are having?" I said, "you can tell me, but I already know it's a boy. I called my belly a boy the whole 9 months. I knew in my gut then my baby was a boy."

I just felt the whole time that my baby was a boy. I wouldn't even go in the girl section in the store when I would go shopping. I just knew, just felt it, and that is the same way I feel about these vitamins and these juices. Before I went with these vitamins and juices, I had thought about doing the dairy-free, yeast-free, gluten-free diet. But that plan wasn't going to work for my son because he would only eat a few items anyway, so if I take all that out, what's left? Nothing but crackers and water. Just saying, now I did try to cut back on his milk, and I didn't mind doing the gluten-free. You really don't miss that in food anyway. That's why I say you have to do what's best for your kids. Only you know your own kids like I said earlier, but he never had stomach problems. The only time he had stomach problems was when he was born, and they gave him that milk, the infant milk, and it didn't agree with his system. That was the only time he had problems with his stomach.

I had to come up with another plan. Wheat-free, gluten-free diet, seems to me, was a plan for kids who had a lot of stomach problems. I was happy I never got rid of my health books. I was happy that I opened my mouth and got my son help early, and I was happy about talking to people about my situation because you never know what advice they give you. With your kid having autism, you can't be ashamed.

It's nothing you did wrong or didn't do. I had to learn that for myself. Don't be ashamed because I always tell people if they have the honor of meeting my son, and he just all of sudden start spinning you will not have those questions that people ask, "Why is he doing that? Why is he shaking these beads like that?" If they already know what's going on, then they would not have to ask, and maybe they will not stare so hard or say something rude. My son loves beads. Everybody who knows him know that he loves beads, and he always has something in his hands. I call whatever he has in his hands, his comforters. It keeps him calm. I let people know who are, close to us. Close friends and family. I let them know that he do have Autism and that's why he does this or that. That's why he spins have something in his hands always, and not talking much. I am not just going to go and tell everybody on the street, but people who are close to us, and people who cares about us.

His behavior used to be so bad when he was two years old. He would get mad sometimes and want to throw things. This was before pre-K, and I told the speech therapist that too. I said he would get so mad and throw his chair to his little table, and he would have to go to time-out. He stayed in time-out. I don't know if that was a sign for autism or if that was just him I can't blame everything on autism, and if we did anything that wasn't in the normal routine, man! He would have a fit every day when he started school. He would get off the bus and run and play, but if he couldn't do that, if I had to go to the store, man! He would cry all the way to the store, and in the store, but that's the whole problem. Kids with autism want to do things the same way and the same things every day. They want the same routine every day, no different. That's not life. That's not how life is. If I need to go to the store to get something for dinner, I can't go, because he is going to have a fit. No, I am going to the store. He had to get out of that fast because there's always something going on around here, so

On the Road to Saying Bye to Autism

if I got something to do, I am doing it, and he will be crying in the store, and I know people was like, "I wish he shut up," and then some people would come up to us and be like, "What's wrong, man? Why you crying?"

Just like one time it was me, his dad, and him. We all went to Applebee's, and usually we would get him a high chair. He was like one or two years old, so the waitress said, "Y'all want a high chair for him?" I said, "No, we will do a booster seat this time." They gave us a seat for him, and he was up and down twisting and turning, couldn't sit still for nothing at all. I could barely enjoy my food. There was this lady looking at us the whole time. I said to his dad, "If that lady looks over here one more time, I'm going to say something." The whole time we were there she was looking at us. I wanted to say so bad, "What are you looking at?" That's how hard she was looking at us.

We are not going to stay in the house just because we don't know how he is going to act in public. We just will not. If you see us in the store and he is crying, my bad, but I needed to go to the store. Turn your head and don't look at us. My kid is not the only kid in the store crying or in a restaurant crying, and I know when people read this book, they will probably say and think I wouldn't take him out every time he's acting like that. But how will they learn how to act in public if you don't take them out. But he has come so far from that, and I know when people read this book. They are probably going to say I wouldn't take him out if he is acting up every time. But how are you going to know if you don't take your kids out? The next time your kid might be the perfect angel. I am not about to be in the house every weekend because I am scared he might act up. If I was like that, we would never go anywhere. But he is so past all that. I would take him out as much as I could, and if he acted up we would tell him right then "You can't do that. You can't act like that."

I learned the more we got him out the better he acted in public. We needed to get him out as often as we could, so he could be around other kids, and adults like at Chuck E. Chesse, and the mall, and at parks he needed to be around other people, so keeping him in the house wasn't gonna help him; plus he always loved to go somewhere. The homework I had him doing for the summer of 2016 was homework I made up. I wrote out his ABCs, and I had written down numbers 1 through 20, and I did the colors the same way, just the main colors— red, green, blue etc. I wrote the word *red*, and next to it a red box that I drew and colored. I would ask him, "What color is this?" So we would go over his colors, his numbers, his shapes, his ABCs, and then I would have him write something, like his name or his numbers. And we did that every evening Monday through Friday. He got used to it when I got off work around 6:00 p.m. I worked from 12:00 to 5:30 p.m. or 6:00 p.m.-12:00 p.m. in the afternoon I would play with him for an hour or so, and then we would get right to work on our homework. Two months is a long time to be out of school without doing some type of homework.

I remember one day we had a meeting at his school, and I talked to his speech therapist. I said one day I asked LaDainian if he was ready to take a bath. He told me no. I asked her, "Do you think he understands what I am asking him?" And she said yeah he understood she said, "Because you have a routine in your house, and he understands the house routine. But you have to explain to him why he needs to take a bath." I was so happy that he had finally answered a question I asked him. He was like three or four years old. I always ask him questions, hoping he would answer. I was so happy that we were finally on a routine, and my little family finally had some structure, no more going to bed at 11 or 12 o'clock at night.

One day I asked him, "LaDainian, you want a little brother or sister?" He said brother. He was six years old at the time. I waited a couple of days. I said, "LaDainian, you want a little brother or sister?" He said again, "Little brother." Well, he just said brother, but sometimes I would just ask him things just to see what he would say. He knew what he was talking about then, and I would like to give him a brother or sister. My brothers got on my nerves growing up, but I was glad they were there, so I wanted that for him. We never wanted him to be the only child. Two is enough, and plus we already got the names picked out for the second one. I think he would be a great big brother.

I came up with another way to get my son to get these vegetables that he is supposed to be eating. I decided to come up with a muffin, a cornbread muffin. He always liked bread and dinner rolls and cornbread, so I came up with this idea, but I didn't do all the vegetables. If I would have done the kale and spinach, it probably would have turned my muffins green. And if they turn any color other than what a regular muffin looks like he will not eat it these muffins are not for kids with a yeast-free, dairy-free, wheat-free diet. Like I said, you have to do what's best for your kid. These vitamins, and juice are working for him along with prayer and a whole lot of thinking. When his grandma made muffins for him at her house, he would be standing by the stove door, waiting on them to finish. He loves them. You can read in the back of this book how I made my muffins. As far as vegetables, I didn't want the color of the muffins to change too much. I just did an apple, pear, banana, cinnamon muffin. If you want to make them a little sweet, you can add honey not sugar. This was my first time making muffins this way. I bought store-brand cornbread mix. I had to come up with all kinds of ways to get him to eat. I had to do what I had to do, and this might sound crazy, but it is the truth.

We have been buying pull-ups until now. I think he was 6 years old. Potty Training usually takes place at like 2 or 3 years old. At that age, LaDainian didn't even know what a potty was. He didn't even understand me when I would ask him "do you have to potty?" He would just look at me like "what is that?" Now, I can tell him and I've done this one morning as soon as he woke up, I said, "LaDainian, go potty, and he went right in there, and did what he had to do. And I might be wrong. But I feel I couldn't teach him how to potty if he doesn't even understand what a potty is. What is a toilet? Everytime I asked him "do you have to potty?", he would say no. He gets his yes and no's mixed up sometimes. It's gotta be a yes in there sometimes. That's why we just would take him every so often. He couldn't tell me when he has to go. Every so often, I would have to take him. And I just gave up. I got tired of doing that. I am not gonna lie, I just gave up. I said he will wear these pull-ups until he understands. I would tell him to go potty, and sometimes, he would look at me like I am crazy.

He was going to first grade 2016–2017 school year. They're not going to change his pull-up. If you take him, he will go. If you tell him to go potty, he will go. You might have to help him with his belt, but he can go, and he was doing great with it. He had on a pull-up when he went to bed at night, but all during the day he had on underwear, and when we went out, he had on the pull-up, but even doing the night he didn't use the bathroom.

In his sleep he will be dry most of the time. He was finally getting it, thank God, and he would do the same at his grandparents' house— underwear in the house and pull-ups out. That seems to be working

On the Road to Saying Bye to Autism

for him along with prayer. Well, this might be getting off the subject a little, but when I was carrying my son, I found out I had fibroids. I didn't know I had them before then, so one day I went online, and I googled the natural way to get rid of fibroids. The first vitamin that popped up I went with that one. And it had great reviews. I don't know what it is in these vitamins, but they are awesome. I asked the doctors, "How did I get them?" They said, "Well, we don't know where they came from or how you get them, but three out of five women have them." It was very painful carrying my son. Read more in first book "The Truth You Didn't Know."

I knew I had to get rid of them somehow. And it wasn't going to be with no surgery—that's for sure. I wasn't about to have surgery on my uterus because that's where I had them at, and doctors don't even know where they come from or how you get them. Surgery is not the answer for everything. That's just how I feel. No offense to doctors, y'all do a great job, but I would like to have more kids, and I don't want to take no chances of that not happening. I ordered me a bottle, and they were great. There's a commercial that come on TV about fibroids, and the lady was packing up pads and all kinds of stuff just to go out, and I said to myself, "That's me packing up to go to war." Go to war with my own body. It sucks. I just got tired of bleeding like a fish every month and in pain the whole time. There had to be a better way, and don't cough or sneeze. You will bleed more. You bleed very heavy with fibrous. One time I got sick with a cold, and my cycle was on too, at the same time. The more I cough and sneeze, the more I was bleeding.

They got the right stuff in these vitamins. My fiborous had got so big. If I put on a slim dress or slim top, it looks like I am about 5 months pregnant. The fiborous made my navel stick out also. I had to get rid of them. I needed some help ASAP. And I wanted help the natural way. I didn't want to have surgery. That wasn't the answer for me. I remember when I was twelve years old I started getting my cycle. I never had any cramps until I turned fifteen. Then when I turned seventeen, eighteen years old, my cramps got really bad. One time they were so bad I sat in the living room chair all day. They didn't start being less painful until I got on birth control. I said, "Man, I should have been on these years ago." I didn't get on birth control until I was in my twenties, and they helped, but it's always a but. But I was 20 pounds overweight. They really made me eat. Fiborous could have come from birth control. I didn't get off birth control until I was out my mama's house in 2005. I wanted to give my body a rest from them, and then I started to lose a little weight, and then I got pregnant with my son in 2009, but doctors don't know where they come from. All I knew was I want to get rid of them. After I had him I bled very heavily. I will be so cold around the house when my cycles on. That's how much blood I think I was losing the first four days it would be on. I hated to leave the house, and when I was a preteen, teenager, I never was heavy like that, but I would be in a lot of pain. Once I got on birth control, they helped with the pain. I wish they would help for bleeding so heavy. If so, I would have been like "Sign me up, put me at the top of the list."

The summer of 2016 was so busy for us. I was trying to make sure I got LaDainian out as much as I could over the summer break. Then he had summer school. I had to make sure he was taking his vitamins every day, and I was working with him on potty training, we had a full summer. We had summer school, potty training, plus I was working part-time and working on this book. I had my hands full this summer. But it was fun. I was determined to have my son ready for first grade and completely potty-trained. I didn't want him to forget nothing he had learned from the school year before. I wanted his teacher to see that he was progressing. I had a hard time in school, and I didn't want the same for my son. You can read more about my school days in my first book, *The Truth You Didn't Know*. I always said if I ever had kids they wouldn't have to worry about nothing but being a kid, because once you're grown, that's it. I want LaDainian to stay a kid as long as he could. Sometimes I wish I was a kid again. I think we all do sometimes. I'll be watching him play sometimes, and he would be having himself a ball. Having fun all by himself. No worries whatsoever. The summer of 2016 was busy, but I couldn't wait for school to start back again because LaDainian still would wake up early no matter how late he went to bed.

I remember when I was in school we didn't have as many breaks as they do now here! They get spring break a week, fall break a week, Thanksgiving a week, Christmas two weeks—really! We didn't get a week for Thanksgiving; we got two days. We didn't get a fall break; they be out too much. But they say the breaks help the students with them taking a break from school like that. I wish we would have had breaks like that, but then our parents would have been complaining just like I am right now. By the end of the summer break, I was tired. I was working part-time. Then I had to take care of LaDainian, making sure he was in one piece. Then I had the house to take care of. On top of that, I was writing this book. How I had time for all that I don't know. I made time. It was hard. That's us women—we just do what we got to do. I'd be so tired by the end of the night. By 11:00 p.m. it's like I took a sleeping pill. I can barely hold my eyes open. I'm so tired. Sometimes I can hardly get in the shower to wash my ass. Some nights I don't even make it. I had a family member ask me, "How did you have time to write a book?" She was talking about my first book, *The Truth You Didn't Know*. But I mostly write at night when the house is quiet and my son asleep. It's too much that goes on in the daytime around here to write anything in the day. Plus, most of the time, I am at work during the day. Now when my son is in school and when I'm off, I can write all day until he gets out of school, but I couldn't do that over the summer break. He stopped taking naps at two years old, so I couldn't write during his naptime. Even when he was in day care or pre-K, he didn't take a nap. He would just lay on his mat quietly. Nighttime writing works for me, unless he is sick with a cold or something. That is the only time he will take a nap.

Well, like I said in the beginning, I am not a doctor or a herbalist. I just did some research to help my son's brain to turn on to the right channel. He was doing much better. He was saying more words and trying to get them together. By June 29, 2016, he still was spinning and very active. But I kept on giving him his vitamins, his corn muffins, the juice. I believed that the vitamins, juice, and muffins would get that channel on. Just within a month time we started seeing improvements, our hard work really started to pay off, and I was so happy. It was hard work, but I knew one day that channel was going to be on, and I was going to have the biggest party for him because we all were waiting to hear that channel up loud, and nonstop talking. The potty training he finally was getting the hang of—thank God. I was spending $12 every two weeks on pull-ups. He was sleeping longer in his bed, but still not all night. I came up with the juice for him because I was tired of feeding him the same things every day. There had to be a better way. He had the juice, the muffins, his vitamins, and his PediaSure. If he wasn't going to eat his fruits and vegetables, then he will drink them, then he's going to eat them in a muffin. Like I said before, I had to stay two steps ahead of him.

The research I did was best for my kid. You have to do what is best for your kid. This plan I came up with was helping him, and it might also help your family. I hope and pray that it does. But like I said before, it's going to take a whole lot of praying and thinking. Maybe one day, I will write a book on LaDainian, an updated book on his progress with all the research. I did a lot of praying and thinking of ways to help my son eat better, and how to get him to take these vitamins. I knew that all my hard work will pay off, and I know your hard work will pay off too.

Lakisha Marie Mackie

"First Family Picture. Done by: Shawn Don"

THINGS THE READERS WILL WANT TO KNOW

APRIL 25, 2016

LaDainian started on his B12, plus an omega-3 fish oil (mercury-free). After that day, on April 27, 2016, LaDainian slept in his bed all night. He has been coming in my bed every night for years. He has not slept in his own bed since he was an infant. That day he didn't come in my room until 4:30 a.m., and I said to myself, "Yes, the vitamins are working. It had to be the vitamins."

APRIL 30, 2016

LaDainian is still coming in my bed at night around the same time, 4:30 a.m., but I have a book on healing foods, and I've been doing my own research on finding foods that will heal his brain and get him talking. Talking and answering questions. Monday to Friday I have been given him his B12 vitamins and his omega-3 fish oil (mercury-free.) I mix it in his regular vitamins that he had been taking since he was two years old. I started him out taking the vitamins with his PediaSure, but he didn't like it. I guess he could smell the fish oil in it, so I ended up putting them in his regular vitamins, which is liquid, and I did it without him seeing me. If he sees me mixing his vitamins, I will have a hard time getting him to take them.

MAY 2, 2016

I have a book on *Natural Medicine*. I looked up learning disabilities, and I found out my son was supposed to be taking more than just B12 and omega-3 fish oil (mercury-free). He was supposed to be taking B12, B6, zinc, copper vitamin, niacin, iodine, omega-3 fish oil (mercury-free), iron, magnesium, manganese, potassium. I found out that all those vitamins help with restoring your brain, and most of these vitamins he was getting in his Poly-Vi-Sol vitamins.

But these vitamins only go to the age of four. So yeah, he was getting them, but it wasn't enough for him once he turned five years old. He is now six years old and still is taking the same vitamins. He would not take any other kind, so my plan was to try and give him the vitamins two ways and see which way work the best. He likes these juices with the different characters like Thomas or Superman. I buy him those juices, and some of them are mixed with vegetables and fruits. First plan was to crush the vitamins up and mix them up with his polyvisol. it would be like a powder, mix it with the liquid vitamins. Second plan was to crush the vitamins up and put it in his juice. Just the crushed vitamins, not the fish oil. And hopefully, he wouldn't taste anything different in his juice. I didn't do the fish oil in the juice, because you can smell the fish oil. And he really will not drink it then and the zinc he got that after school on a full stomach. Because zinc can sometimes upset your stomach. Unless he ate breakfast before he went to school like on Fridays, I would give him the zinc vitamin after he ate breakfast on Fridays before he went to school. Because he had speech therapy before school on Fridays. If not, it will make your stomach upset. You will feel like you got to throw up. I added a third plan. The third plan was to make him smoothies with fruit and vegetables that have the same vitamins that he needs. Fruits and

On the Road to Saying Bye to Autism

vegetables have vitamins in them also. So that's how I was able to pick what fruit and vegetables he needs. But the third plan didn't work. He didn't like the smoothies. I had to stay two steps ahead of him always. I wanted to give him all his vitamins in the morning before school and get it out the way. That way I know he got all his vitamins for the day, but with the juice and the smoothies I had to sit and make sure he sits, and drink all of it. It was a job that I was willing to do. I couldn't put the fish oil, and the other vitamins in his juice because he wouldn't want it. I didn't want him to not like the juice no more so I stopped that, that day because he didn't like the juice with the vitamins in it. When I put that fish oil in his PediaSure, and he could smell it, and didn't want it, I stopped that, that day. He had been taking the vitamins great. Before then. Yeah, he would fight a little, because it's nasty, and no kid want to take anything nasty. But he took them like a sport. I want to help my son the natural way. Not medicine from a doctor where he would be like a zombie all day long. Medicine is not the only answer for everything—no offense. I read this one book. This lady was giving her son B12 shots. Now I couldn't bring myself to do that, so I just did the B12 vitamins. The shots probably work the fastest, but I just couldn't do that, and the vitamins work just as well, just not as fast.

MAY 4, 2016

LaDainian is still sleeping in his bed all night til about 4:30 a.m., so I felt like I was getting somewhere. Then he woke up this morning just yelling out words he had been yelling out words for the last couple of days. He had been saying more words way before I started the fish oil and the B12. I just needed those words to come together and make a sentence.

MAY 6, 2016

This is the second week since I've been given LaDainian his B12 and his fish oil omega-3 fish oil (mercury-free). I had read that kids with autism is supposed to be on a wheat-free, yeast-free, dairy-free diet—some kind of way yeast from like breads could stay in your stomach and it's not healthy if you can't move it out. But my son never had problems going to the bathroom. The only time he had problems with his bowels was when he had colic when he was a newborn/infant from the milk he was given, so I didn't do the yeast-free, wheat-free diet. I did ease up on giving him milk, because he was getting milk in his PediaSure too. The book I read said kids with autism should also be on a gluten-free, wheat free diet. I am also saying to myself he is already not eating much of nothing. For breakfast, he likes pancakes, waffles, grits, oatmeal, turkey bacon, sausage links. Breakfast wasn't a problem. It was dinner that was the problem. Because all he wanted for dinner was nuggets, fries, pizza, cheeseburgers, grill cheese, peanut butter and jelly sandwiches I had a hard time trying to get him to eat.

MAY 9, 2016

I started LaDainian on the rest of his vitamins today, and I didn't just start him on all the vitamins at one time. I kind of spread them out. I gave him a little at a time. Like the B12 and the omega-3 fish oil he just took those for two weeks straight, just those two. I just didn't want to give him all those vitamins at one time, plus it can get expensive. When you want your child healthy, you will spend the money. The next group of items I bought were zinc, B6, and the magnesium. I wasn't getting a good feeling about the copper or the iodine. You could do copper and iodine if you'd like, but I didn't, and the zinc, I gave that to him when he got home from school since his belly would be full. The fish oil was 1,000 mg. I wouldn't give him that much, only half, and the B12 was 1,000 mg. I would give him a half of a half because if not he will grow wings and fly away. He would have so much energy. The zinc was 50 mg, so I would give him half of that. The B6 was 100 mg, so he would get half of a half, and last, magnesium, was 250 mg. He would get half of a half every day, Monday through Friday, and I would just sit and watch him and let his body get used to those first before I started on the other. So the first two weeks he got the fish oil and B12. On the second two weeks, he got the zinc, the B12, and fish oil. Only the zinc in the afternoon, the rest of them was in the morning, before he went to school, so I am giving these items to him a little at a time because I don't want to hurt him, and I don't want him to get sick. The potassium you can get from bananas. I did the research, and all the vitamins he was supposed to be taking I couldn't give him all at one time. It was like 12 vitamins altogether, including the copper and the iodine. But I didn't go with the copper and iodine. If I don't feel right or good about something, I don't do it, and I didn't give him any vitamins on the weekend because I wanted to give his body a rest. I don't believe the vitamins can hurt you, but the weekends I just want him to rest from them. It's not like the vitamins are just going to leave his system, so for two or three weeks he will get just the fish oil, B12, zinc, magnesium, B6, and then he will get the other three or four later, rather than just giving him all of them at one time. Like I said, vitamins can be expensive once they add up, but I feel giving him a little at a time will be good for him.

MAY 10, 2016

I ended up putting a zinc vitamin in his PediaSure at night, and he would have it when he gets home from school. I had hoped that the zinc would melt or something. When I put the B12 like that, it just went to the top of the bottle, and you can see it at the top. I guess I didn't crush it up enough.

MAY 11, 2016

I gave LaDainian his zinc in his PediaSure, and it worked. You can't even see it in there, nor could he tell. I like giving him his vitamins during the day while he was in school, that way he could burn off the extra energy he had during the day and when he was out of school for the summer. I did the same thing. He had been trying to put more and more words together.

MAY 12, 2016

LaDainian had started putting some weight on him, which was a good thing because he had lost some weight when he had got the flu during the winter. He needed that weight back. He is never still, so he would never be fat. He always running around. I found out some of the vitamins was in his PediaSure that LaDainian needed to help repair his brain. Some of them were in his PediaSure. The magnesium I had bought was 250 mg, so I was only giving him a pinch of that. He got 10 percent in the PediaSure, 10 percent magnesium, 30 percent B6, iodine 15 percent, niacin 10 percent. Potassium he was getting 350 mg at 15 percent all in his PediaSure. PediaSure is lactose free suitable for lactose intolerance. I never gave him regular milk ever

On the Road to Saying Bye to Autism

since he started drinking regular milk. When it was time for him to drink regular milk at one year old, he got the Lactaid milk. Even as an infant we had to switch his milk, so what I did was I just let him keep getting the potassium and the magnesium in his PediaSure. I was told not to overdo it with the potassium. The vitamins that I bought was the B12, omega-3 fish oil (mercury-free), magnesium, zinc, B6. I had a hard time trying to find the thiamine and the niacin. But the niacin he also got in PediaSure. I still didn't buy the copper or the iodine, so I have come up with another plan to let the Poly-Vi-Sol go because the PediaSure and the vitamins that I was buying were enough. I didn't want to overdo it. The iron, I could buy that separate too, so during the summer, I crush up all his vitamins and put them all in his PediaSure. During the summer we weren't on any schedule, so he had all day to drink that PediaSure, so my advice would be to give your child the PediaSure, especially if your child is a picky eater like mine. I know some people say that yeast-free, gluten-free, wheat-free diet works too, but after you take all that away, what's left? My kid is already not eating enough. That's why I didn't go with that diet plan. I had to do what was best for us, and he had been saying more and more words since he has been taking the extra vitamins.

MAY 13, 2016

I heard LaDainian saying some new words today. I'm so happy. I think I'm on the right road.

MAY 15, 2016

I did more research, and I found some fruits and vegetables that LaDainian is supposed to be eating to help him. These fruits and vegetables also help hyperactive children to calm them down. LaDainian is very active, so my plan was to come up with a juice that he would drink only on the weekends since he had his vitamins and PediaSure during the week. I wasn't giving him the vitamins on the weekend, so it was seventeen different fruits and vegetables—pears, broccoli, cucumbers, carrots, yams, squash, cabbage, oranges. My plan was to come up with a juice that I think he will love and taste good. At first I thought about doing a smoothie, and I did but he didn't like it. It wasn't thin enough. He hated the smoothie, but it was good, I liked it. I brought a juicer and made him one juice instead of doing two juices they are in this book also.

1st juice	2nd juice	Juice I made
Spinach, oranges	Kale	Kale, spinach, pear
Bananas	Apple	Apple, blueberries
Yams	Blueberries	Oranges, broccoli
Cabbage	Celery	Carrots, squash
Strawberries	Pears	Strawberries
Cucumbers	Broccoli	Cucumbers
Cherries	Squash	Cherries only add a handful
Carrots	cherries	Cabbage,

I used kale, spinach, strawberries, blueberries, cucumbers, oranges, carrots, apple, pears, broccoli, squash, cherries, and an all-natural honey as a sweetener. Now they didn't have kale on the list, but I like how kale makes you feel when you eat it, so I added kale.

The research I did say he needs high in green vegetables like spinach. So of course, if I made a meal out of these vegetables he wouldn't want to eat it. Like I said before, anything outside of nuggets, pizza, fries, if it's not that kind of stuff, he doesn't want it. I had to make a juice out of it and put it in his juice bottle and give it to him. That way as long as I would make it taste good it shouldn't be a problem. I used the juice bottle that I was talking about with the different characters. I would take the juice out of the bottle and put it in a regular cup, put the juice I made in the juice bottle. I had to do what I had to do. I have to stay two steps ahead of him always. If he would have seen me put anything in that bottle besides what supposed to be in that juice bottle, he wouldn't want it. I would do the juice at night while he was sleep. He had his vitamins and his juice. He was gaining weight, which was good because the vitamins were making him eat. I added honey to the juice sometimes when the juice wasn't sweet enough. Honey is better for you instead of sugar.

MAY 19, 2016

I noticed that LaDainian eye contact has gotten better. Kids with Autism don't like to look at people in their eyes. Even when you are talking to them. This is what my research said, each fruit and vegetables had in them. And this is how I was able to pick what fruit and vegetables he is supposed to have. These fruits and vegetables have the same vitamins that he needs to help his brain.

1. Blueberries – potassium, manganese, magnesium, iron, niacin

2. Broccoli – is an excellent source of vegetarian iron

3. Oranges – vitamin C, potassium

4. Spinach – iron, magnesium, manganese, and zinc

5. Banana's – has potassium

6. Apples – are high in fiber, and pectin both promote bowel regularity

7. Cabbage – excellent source of many nutrients, vitamin C, potassium, folic acid, vitamins B6, biotin, calcium, magnesium, and manganese

8. Celery – is rich in potassium and sodium. Celery is a good source of calcium, folic acid, B6, B1, vitamin B2 capable of enhancing the activity of certain white blood cells

9. Cucumbers – is a very good source of vitamin C, and A and folic acid

10. Carrots – provide excellent levels of vitamin K, biotin, and fiber, and very good levels of vitamins C, and B6, potassium, and thiamine

11. Strawberries – has vitamins C and K, dietary fiber, flavonoids, manganese, and iodine, B6

12. Kale – excellent source of vitamins C, B6, and manganese, B1, B2, and E. Includes many minerals, copper, iron, and calcium

13. Pears – are an excellent source of water. They are also a good source of vitamin C, copper, B2 and E, and potassium

14. Cherries – Good source in vitamins A and C, and copper and manganese

MAY 22, 2016

The vitamins that I was giving LaDainian was giving him life. I feel he was gaining weight. He was looking better. He is already cute. And he still had three vitamins that he was supposed to be taking that I hadn't brought yet. These vitamins were doing him some good. He also was saying more and more new words. He went in his room one day he said, "My Bed" I said, "Yes, this is your bed." I had never heard him say that. And one day he was sitting on the couch, and he started saying the days of the week. They talk about that in school. Well, they say their days of the week in school. I never know what might come out his mouth these days.

MAY 23, 2016

LaDainian slept in his room all night last night. Until about 4:30 am. I think I am getting somewhere. Even if he just slept in his bed all night twice a week that's more than he done in years. He was really coming along. I noticed that LaDainian would look at me in my eyes, but he still wouldn't look at people in their faces. When they were talking to him. We would have to tell him to look at the person, because he would turn around away from the person who was talking to him. And we would have to tell him to turn around. I prayed that, that would get better. If he could look at my eyes, he could look at other people eyes. I felt.

MAY 27, 2016

May 25, 2016 made a month since I had been giving LaDainian his vitamins. And he had been doing very well. Gaining weight, looking better, trying to say more new words, and this was all in a month time.

MAY 29, 2016

LaDainian was trying more and more to put his words together. And I was doing more and more praying and thinking. My goal was to get that channel cut on in his brain. I needed that part of his brain to be on the right channel. And I wanted him talking and answering questions this year 2016. When he graduated from kindergarten. He was singing along with the other kids. I was so proud. The school year before he was crying the whole time. He was singing in his own little way. But he wasn't crying, and he did great.

MAY 30, 2016

LaDainian had come home from Florida this day with his grandparents. He had been gone a week. This week he only had his vitamins Monday, Tuesday, and Wednesday. We had to get back on track, just because school was out didn't mean we was going to stop our routine. He was still going to get his vitamins Monday–Friday along with his PediaSure and his juice on the weekends. And we were still going to have our summer school right here at home. I read to him at night, at bedtime, and when I got off work in the evening time we had homework. Because I didn't want him to forget what he had learned during the school year. He didn't like doing the homework, but he got used to it. It had to be done. The next school year he was going to first grade. And I wanted him to be ready. Plus, he had his V-Tech games. That talks to him. And this game he has teaches. The days of the week, counting, ABC's, and he was playing with that every day. I was able to give him his zinc vitamin in the day too. Since he was out of school. Because I gave him his vitamins after breakfast, every morning. Like I said before in this book, zinc can make your stomach upset. If you take it on an empty stomach. And I didn't want him to be sick.

JUNE 1, 2016

On this day LaDainian made me so happy. He was going to the restroom by himself. Now at his grandparents' house he would go by his self all the time. But at home *never*. We would have to keep taking him. Since he wasn't telling us when he had to go. We struggle with potty training for years. But this day he had just kept going on his own. I guess he was finally getting it. I was so proud. I prayed so hard this day. I said, "Please let him keep going on his own. Every day, all day." I said it had to be the vitamins he was taking, that was helping that part of his brain. Because he was finally getting it. If he was going to go on his own without telling me that's fine too. You know what the toilet is for now. I kept telling myself, *it got to be the vitamins.* He had never gone to the bathroom like that on his own. Maybe only one other time. That I can remember. I said to myself, *I am on the right track.*

JUNE 2, 2016

LaDainian did keep going to the restroom on his own on this day. Like he had done the day before. But I kept giving him his vitamins and praying and thinking.

JUNE 5, 2016

LaDainian went to the restroom again by himself. And he hadn't done that no more since June 2. He did it again this day. And that made me proud. He was able to go without me taking him every hour or so. We had a busy summer this summer. Even though he didn't have ESY (Extended School Year). This summer we had ESY at home. Monday to Friday was home work and learning. Along with taking vitamins and practicing going to the restroom on his own. Saturday and Sundays were family time. Really Sunday was, since me and his dad was off on Sundays. Family time and drinking juice time.

JUNE 6, 2016

LaDainian slept in his own bed all night last night. And like I said earlier in this book he didn't do that too often. I needed him to do that every night. And go to the restroom on his own every day.

JUNE 8, 2016

LaDainian still was making progress. This day we didn't do homework. We had took LaDainian for a ride, me and his dad. But LaDainian and his dad was counting in the car. We didn't go the whole day without learning something this day. I didn't want to go to many days with missing homework. Because we were on a role. He was doing good with his numbers, and colors, and shapes. I didn't want him to forget nothing. I wanted him to be ready for first grade and talking. And he was getting there. Plus, he had his GPB channel on T.V. too. I felt really good about everything that I was doing to help my son.

JUNE 10, 2016

LaDainian still was doing great saying more words and sleeping in his bed longer. He still was coming in my bed around 4:00 am every night. He was starting to get used to doing that homework in the evenings. He didn't get much homework for kindergarten, but over the summer (2016). I had plenty of homework for him. He got use to taking them vitamins too.

JUNE 13, 2016

LaDainian was doing great the summer of 2016. I tried to get him out as much as I could over the summer break. I wanted him to be around as many kids and adults, as I could. He needed to be around other people besides us. With him being the only child he needed to get out. The more I could get him to Chuck E. Chesse and to Parks, the better for him.

JUNE 15, 2016

LaDainian was doing great. This day he went to the bathroom all day. And didn't have one accident. He had been wearing pull-ups up to this day. Because he still was having accidents. And some days still I had to take him. But at his grandparents' house he went on his own all the time. Why he couldn't do that at home, I don't know. I had taken him this day to the playground, and even at the playground he didn't have an accident. I was letting him wear pull-ups while we are out, but underwear in the house. And that seem to be working. He was going to the first grade 2016 and 2017 school year. He couldn't go with a pull-up on. We had the whole summer to get it down pack. And I knew he could do it. It was time.

JUNE 17, 2016

LaDainian was doing great with the potty training. Some days he would go on his own. We had a lot of things to get done for the summer of 2016. Speech, potty training, and practicing what he learns during the school year. And still have fun at the same time.

JUNE 19, 2016

LaDainian was doing great with the potty training and saying more words. He was still taking his vitamins Monday to Friday, and homework Monday to Friday. This day he had went to the restroom by his self a couple of times. Family and friends was seeing a lot of improvement in him. And that was just from extra vitamins. And you know we talk to him, read to him, just take up as much time as we could with him. And that helps out a lot too. We try to get him out as often as we can.

JUNE 24, 2016

LaDainian was still doing great. He had a few accidents with the potty training. But he was getting the hang of it. When I first started him on his Juice he didn't like it. I had put it in my Blender, so it came out more like a smoothie. And it wasn't thin enough, so he didn't like it. I had to invest in a juicer and start all over again with the juice with a juicer machine. And he still didn't like it. But it's all good. I still make him drink it anyway.

JUNE 26, 2016

I had noticed that LaDainian wasn't' spinning that much no more. I just happen to think about it, when I was watching him play this day. I had said if these vitamins could get the spinning, the holding my ears, to none, or not as much. I would be happy. When he was in Pre-K he had to have a weighed cap on his head. Because he liked that pressure on his head. And he had to have like a weighed vest, or it was something they would put on his lap. To help him keep still in his seat in class. And his teacher and his speech therapist said it worked. When he was in kindergarten he didn't need none of that. No weighed cap, no weighed vest. He was getting better. I was hoping for my next plan to work. Buy this juicer and make this juice. And work on these muffins. One way or another he was gonna get these fruits and vegetables in him.

JUNE 29, 2016

LaDainian was still spinning but it was not that much. Which I was happy about that. But I did notice him starting to get more of an attitude. If I tell him no you can't have that. Anytime I said no, he would try to throw something, or try to hurt me and his dad. Because he mad. That's just like in the beginning when we first started getting him help. I don't know why he was going back to having an attitude like that again. He would get mad when he was 2 and 3 years old, and just throw something. But potty training was going good still. Using less and less pull-ups. Half of the time he had started going by himself. We were still doing the vitamins Monday to Friday. And homework since school was still out at this time. But I did give him breaks in between. He was saying more and more words, gaining weight, and getting taller. I was trying my very best to get him ready for first grade. He also was still coming in my room at night to get in my bed. I would pray every night that he would sleep in his bed all night.

JULY 2, 2016

LaDainian was still doing great. He still was giving us attitude. I am not sure why he is going back to that stage. But I knew how to get him out of that, make him sit down and put him in time out he hates that. He hates sitting down not doing nothing. But all the other things he was doing good at. Trying to talk, potty training, his homework. But that attitude had to go. He's spoiled, I know that, and I take blame for that but that's still no reason to be bad.

JULY 5, 2016

LaDainian said a full sentence yesterday. They were firing firecrackers in my neighborhood yesterday. And he was like "It's too loud, it's too loud." Loud noise hurt his ears. And it was pretty loud. We were getting out of the car, and I tried to get him in the house fast as I could. He was doing great with potty training, he just had to get more practice with putting his clothes back on and washing his hands. I was working hard getting him ready for first grade.

JULY 8, 2016

LaDainian had heard somebody on T.V. say you so smart. And he said the same thing just as clear. I just needed that channel to always be on and more often. He was saying sentences, but not all the time. He was just repeating what he heard or hear somebody else say. Sometimes he would say things on his own. But for the most part he will say what you say. And in the beginning, he wasn't doing none of that. When I look back and think when he was 2 and 3 years old, I say man! He has come a long way. And I was so proud.

JULY 9, 2016

LaDainian had started to go to the bathroom by himself. Sometimes I would say, "LaDainian go to the potty," and he would go. And I just go in there to help him when I hear the toilet. But he was doing good in that department. He would still have a few mistakes. And I still didn't trust him to go out without a pull-up on. Especially if we were gonna be gone more than an hour. Of course, I would take him to the restroom, if we was at a restaurant but if we was riding he wasn't telling me, "Momma I have to potty." That's why I would tell him to go potty. And sometimes like I said he was going on his own. If I was expecting around this time, I can't change two people diapers. Hell No!!! Hopefully soon I can say goodbye to pull-ups, 12 dollars can add up.

JULY 12, 2016

LaDainian was doing great. We had taken him to McDonalds this day. And I ordered him some nuggets and the lady were like, what kind of sauce do you need? I said no sauce. He was like no sauce. He had started to repeat everything he had heard us say. And as far as the potty training goes, he was doing great with that. Most of the time he was going on his own. I even took him out a few times with underwear on. But I still wasn't sure if I wanted him to go to school with just underwear. I wasn't too sure about that.

JULY 14, 2016

LaDainian had asked me this morning he said what are you doing? I said, I am getting dressed I gotta go to work. He was doing, so good with his speech. I was so happy. I couldn't' believe he asked me that. At this point we never knew what might come out his mouth. He was doing great. Still coming in my room at night getting in my bed. When will that end? I wonder.

JULY 16, 2016

LaDainian was doing great with the potty training. I was thinking about letting him wear underwear for the first time to school or to school. We had done a few practice runs a few times out. I wanted to see how long he could go without making a mistake of course I would take him to the bathroom while we were out, but he was doing good. That was one of my goals. To get him potty train, now that he understands what a toilet is. And what a toilet was for. Get him potty trained, help him with numbers, shapes, colors, and his ABC's. Those was my goals for him over the summer break of 2016. He was doing good also with those things. We were very proud of him. School was starting back on August 1, 2016. And he had to be ready for it. And I had to make sure he was ready.

JULY 21, 2016

LaDainian was still doing great with the potty training. He would use the restroom, pull his clothes up, and wash his hands and dry them. And I was so happy because we weren't buying no more pull-ups, that was for sure. I know that might be a small thing to most people, but that was big for us. We had been buying pull-ups until now. So he was gone start the year out with wearing underwear. (The new school year). And he was repeating everything we would say, and what he heard on T.V. I just needed him to be able to answer questions. Like if somebody ask how you doing man? I wanted him to say good. But I knew one day he would get to that point. I knew it was coming because he was doing so good. I just wish he would sleep in his bed at night. God, I prayed for that every night. He was starting to get to big for real. He still would sometimes hand me his cup to put something to drink in it. And I would ask him. What do you want? And when he wouldn't say nothing I would just put the cup down. You gotta say what you want.

JULY 24, 2016

LaDainian had school coming up soon. I had to make sure I had all his vitamins, his PediaSure, and everything else. Because he hated the school lunch. He would want the same thing every day, nothing new. I had to also get him back into a routine with school being out, he didn't really have a sleeping routine. I would let him stay up no later than 10:00 pm. He normally would fall out by 9:00 pm. But when school is in bed time is at 8:00 pm. Monday to Friday we try 8:00 pm normally when he first starts school we start out at 8:00 pm, but if he acts like he can't get up we take it back to 7:30 pm. Bed time is at 8:00 pm, he is getting in the shower or bath at 7:00 or 7:30 pm and by 8:00 pm he is in the bed, and I am reading him a story. We go to bed so early, because we are up at 5:30 am. Sometimes after I read him his story I be sleep before him I be so tired. And when I wake up its 11 or 12 o'clock at night. Hadn't took no shower or nothing.

On the Road to Saying Bye to Autism

JULY 29, 2016

LaDainian had open house at his school today. This day we had a chance to meet his new teacher. I told her I said he done so well, last school year that he didn't need ESY (Extended School Year). I said but the whole summer we had ESY at home. I said I didn't want him to forget nothing. His new teacher said, "Oh that's great." I said and also, he is not wearing pull-ups this school year. I said if you take him he will go. I said or if he knows where the restroom is he will go on his own. I said you might look up, and he is gone in the restroom. She said, "Oh that's fine too." I talked about his eating. I said he is still a picky eater. That part has not changed. Overall, I think the summer of 2016 was a great summer. And I think LaDainian had a great summer. Now it's time for him to go back to school and learn as much as he can this new school year.

AUGUST 4, 2016

LaDainian was doing great in school. His grandma had asked him one day. She said how was school? And he said good. She said she was so surprise. And I said I am too. Just hearing that made me happy. She would get him off the school bus while I was at work. And she would take him to her house. But he has never answered a question before. Unless you ask him if he has to go potty? I only remember one other time. I had asked him was he ready to go get in the shower? And he told me, "No." so it's not very often, that he will answer a question. Unless I tell him say yes or say no. When his grandma told me that, I said yeah, it's those vitamins. That speech is gone turn on like you turn on a T.V. That's what happened as far as the potty training. He just all of sudden started going on his own. Once I got on board with his grandma, once he had the same routine he had at his grandma house. He just started going on his own. He was doing good with that because I wasn't buying no more pull-ups. He was going to wear underwear for sure.

AUGUST 8, 2016

LaDainian wasn't eating his lunch good in school. That's what his teacher said on her note that she sent home. I had told her at open house that he was a very picky eater. I sent her a list of things that he likes to eat for lunch and breakfast. They get breakfast in school too. So hopefully that list helps, because he only eats certain things. That's why I have to make sure he has his PediaSure. And his vitamins, and his juice. He needs those PediaSures and vitamins. If he only eats certain things.

AUGUST 10, 2016

LaDainian had told me he said, "Get up." He wanted me to get up off the couch. He was like get up. I said where we going? And he was like night, night. He was ready to go to bed. I said to myself Yup those vitamins are kicking in. He was starting to answer questions more often. And we were so proud of him.

AUGUST 15, 2016

LaDainian told me for the first time yesterday that he had to go potty. He was like "Potty." I said you gotta go potty? We were at a restaurant for dinner yesterday. And he had to go potty. And he actually said potty. That might not be big for most people, but that was big for us. At home he just went when he had to go. But yesterday he told me. Man! Those vitamins are really working. And I was so proud of myself. He was really coming along.

AUGUST 18, 2016

LaDainian was doing great. He was saying more words and trying to answer questions. He was doing great with the potty training. I had refused to buy anymore pull-ups, good nights and whatever else. I was so proud of him.

AUGUST 25, 2016

LaDainian was doing so good in school this school year. With the potty training and all. And one day he was at his grandma house, and she had asked him to go downstairs and go in the kitchen and get pop, pop a bottle water. This was the other day. And he went and did exactly what she said. We never said he couldn't understand what was being said to him. He is a very smart kid. That part of his brain was on the right channel. The part of his brain that needed to be turned on was the speech, and communication part. But I knew that speech was on the way.

AUGUST 27, 2016

LaDainian was doing so good. He told me today he said, "I got kale." I asked him I said "You got kale? No, I said you got what? And he said kale. I said kale, and I just started laughing. Now I never talked to him about nothing about no kale. He probably heard me talk about it with a family member. So, who knows. Every day I see that channel becoming more and more clear every day. One day he is gonna go to bed one night, and wake up, and just start talking. That channel is just gonna turn on, and gonna be all the way clear, and up loud. Just like with the potty training. It just clicks and he just started going on his own. The speech is gonna be the same way. Them vitamins is truly working along with pray.

AUGUST 29, 2016

I never know what LaDainian will say or do these days. Yesterday we went to go look at this house and it had, had a two-door garage and I opened the door to it. And LaDainian was like Hello, Hello, he could hear his echo. I said boy you are a trip. He was really coming along. All my research and praying were really paying off. It was coming up on 5 months since I started his vitamins, so I should be seeing some great progress.

SEPTEMBER 3, 2016

LaDainian would go to his grandma house after school until I get off work. One day he went to her house, and he always try to do things on his own. Like he grown instead of asking for help. He was at her house, and kids that have Autism have their own tune or hum. They like to repeat or sing. His grandparents watching T.V. and they hear him in his room, but he has a different tune this time. His grandma goes in his room, and he saying "Somebody, somebody, somebody." He had got his hand stuck on the side of the T.V. trying to get a DVD that he wanted to watch. He just kept saying somebody, somebody. Boy them words was coming out more and more. That channel is not so dark no more. And LaDainian loves beads. He loves to shake them. His dad had brought him two new beads, and I said LaDainian tell daddy thanks for the beads. And he said it word for word. "Thanks for the beads." I just be in shock everyday of what he is gonna say.

SEPTEMBER 11, 2016

LaDainian was surprising me more and more every day. He was watching his Barney DVD in his room, and he was saying them words. And most of the time I act like I don't hear him, because I be wanting him to keep going. And if I stop and say what did you say? He will stop. He will not keep counting or saying his ABC's. He will get shy.

OCTOBER 18, 2016

LaDainian was doing great, his teacher said. Today we had a teacher parent meeting. And his speech therapist was like what did you do over the summer with him? I said we had summer school at home. I said you don't have ESY this summer, but we gonna have it here at home, and she said she could tell. I said yup we worked real hard over the summer Monday to Friday. They said well, we can see great improvements. They said, but we do want him to get into a speech clinic outside of school. They said if it is only one day a week that will help even more. So once his speech therapist gave me a list of speech clinics I got him sign up to one. Every Fridays before school he goes to speech. He goes every Friday for 30 minutes.

NOVEMBER 6, 2016

LaDainian was doing great. I had ended up signing him up for speech class outside of school. On Fridays we had him go to speech therapy, and then go to school after. The more speech classes he had the better. I was trying my hardest to get him back at his home school. He was getting speech 3 times a week. In school 2 days a week, and outside of school 1 day. And they give him an excuse for school, so it did not count against him. Because he hadn't missed no days of school. I was so proud of him.

NOVEMBER 18, 2016

LaDainian was doing great! He is coming along very well. He was talking more and trying to answer more questions. His teacher sent a note home, and she said he had improved so much. Since the beginning of the school year. So we was happy to hear that. One day I had sneezed, and he said bless you. We always tell him say thank you, say good morning, so everything is finally starting to turn on and I was so happy things was starting to turn around for the better. And him taking the outside speech classes was only gonna help more.

NOVEMBER 22, 2016

Things really was starting to stick with LaDainian. He was getting it. We would tell him if somebody give you something you say thank you. It was starting to stick where he would do it on his own. I had sneezed one day, and LaDainian said, "Bless you." We always tell him say bless you, say thank you, say good morning. It was finally sticking. The more I read to him, the more I repeat things to him the more he was getting it. It was taking time, but he was getting it, and he was making all of us happy and proud.

NOVEMBER 27, 2016

LaDainian was doing so well. I knew in my heart he would be at his old school the next school year. That's how good he was doing. I had heard him this day count on his own from 1–18. And I was doing some house work, so I was acting like I didn't hear him or listening just to see how far he would go. If I act like I am listening, then he will stop. I was saying to myself you go boy. He knows the work. It's just now it's really starting to come out. Finally pray, and never giving up really do work. Which I will never give up. Because it's my child. And I would do anything to help my son. I never gave up on giving him his vitamins, his juice on the weekends and his muffins my main concern was the vitamins and the juice. The muffins were just something to try. And his PediaSure. And whatever else I could research on to help him. We were doing whatever his teacher said would help him at home. We were doing what his speech therapist said in school. She said he should have speech outside of school, so we did that. Every Friday he went to speech class, after speech he went to school. And he hated that part. He hated going to school after speech.

NOVEMBER 28, 2016

We had to go to a IEP meeting, for LaDainian today. And all his teachers say how much he had improved. We found out that he goes to P.E, music, and recess to play with a regular first grade class. And that is big for students with Autism because it's hard for them sometimes to be around other people. So that is huge for him. And me and his dad was so happy to hear that, I know I was. They were worried about the Christmas break. They are out so long during the break. Two weeks. They are worried that he will forget some of the things he learned and some of his speech. But like I told them he will still have the speech classes., at the clinic. Plus, I am always going over some type of homework with him. Because they were saying that if he seems like he don't remember how to count or his ABC's, then he will have to go to ESY, for the summer of 2017. I was trying to reassure them that he will be fine. Our next IEP meeting was the spring of 2017. Which is like a big meeting with all the teachers, his OT therapist, his speech therapist., everybody. And we all talk about his goals, and what he needs to improve in if anything. But he was coming along very well and me and his dad was so proud of him.

DECEMBER 10, 2016

LaDainian was playing on my bed this day he loves to play on my bed, or up under the covers. He was like come on Kisha. He wanted me to get under the covers with him. He just insists on calling me by my first name. sometimes he calls me momma. Like he knows I am his momma. But most of the time he is calling me Kisha. And I know this is gonna be sad to say. But I really don't push the issue. Years ago. I couldn't even get him to say that or anything. And only a parent with a child that have Autism can understand that. (No offense). I am just so happy he is saying something. And it makes you feel so good inside. To hear your child finally talking. It sounds like when you hear your favor song on the radio, that you have not heard in a long time. How good you feel when you hear it. That's what hearing him talk sounds like to me. I really don't care what he calls me. LOL.

DECEMBER 11, 2016

Well, I also wanted to report that ginger help with fibrous. It helps shrink and dissolve them. I had been doing 2 oz. ginger shots for almost 2 mos. by this time. And I was taking it, because I didn't want to get sick over the winter. With a bad cold or flu. I was taking it for that reason. Because it helps build your immune system. It helps with stomach aches and a lot of stomach problems. I did my research and it said ginger helps dissolve and shrinks fibrous. And when my cycle came on for November it was a breeze, I had no idea ginger helped for fibrous, get you some fresh ginger, put it in your blender with a little water then put it in your juicer, and juice it. Then you will do 2 oz. ginger a day and take it back like a shot. And ginger gives you energy too. The vitamins help too. It does the same as the ginger. And that ginger will last a week. Keep cold, always make sure before you take a shot you shake and mix it first. Ginger tend to stick at the bottom of your container. I just wanted to give more information on that. That's what I was doing to help myself. Because I sure wasn't about to have any surgery. And plus, I wanted to have at least one more baby. I needed to get rid of them. I didn't want to be in any pain with carrying a second child like I was with LaDainian. That ginger is gonna burn when you take that shot. And it might be a little spicy. But it is well worth it. After a while you get used to it.

DECEMBER 12, 2016

LaDainian had an appointment today at the speech clinic that I got him sign up to. And today they just tested him. He went on to the back by himself. With the speech therapist. And of course, when you go to any type of clinic for your child (speech wise). You gotta answer all these questions. Does your child do this or that? How many words do you think your child says? And any parent who has a child with Autism knows about all the questions and answers. But it's worth it, if its gonna help your child do great. I say go ahead, and answer those questions. It's not gonna hurt nobody, all it can do is help. Clinics don't care how long it will take you to answer those questions. Help them help your child. You gotta be truthful. I have been at clinics where LaDainian is finished talking to the therapist, before I am finished answering the questions. Starting December 30, 2016 he will be going to this clinic every Friday for 30 minutes. To work on his speech. So, him going on Fridays will be a third day for him during the week. When he is finish on Fridays with his speech classes at the clinic then he will go to school. And they will give him an excuse for school. So, after he was finished today the therapist came out with him and was asking us questions just for her own information, and she said it's so good y'all got him help early. I tell you the earlier the better. That really makes a difference. He has been getting help since he was 3 years old. And by the time he starts his classes at the clinic he will be 7 years old. He will be 7 on the 22 of December. He been getting help by this time for 4 years now. And he really was coming along. I was happy for him.

DECEMBER 17, 2016

LaDainian was surprising me every day and I am not making up any of his progress. We had taken him to the Barbara shop and it was a lady there that had just got her hair done. So, after she was finished it was LaDainian's turn to get his haircut. And we were telling her he had a birthday coming up. We saw her in the shop many times. So, she known us for a while. And she was like what do you want for your birthday? And he was like cake. And me and his dad just looked at each other. Like what!!! He understood what she was saying, and what she was asking him. Then she asked him what was his name? So, he said name? She said yeah name? What's your name? I didn't hear him say his name because she was talking to him while his head was down. He was getting his haircut. I had answered for him. And she said yeah, he told me. He had already said his name. I said man! He has come a long way. Me and his dad was so happy. The lady told him, I guess mom and dad will have to get you that birthday cake. She said you have a good birthday and Christmas LaDainian. I said tell her thank you. And he said thank you. Me and his dad was like man! because we remember when we couldn't get him to say nothing at all. It really takes a team. Everybody have to be on the same page. Family, close friends, doctors, speech therapist, OT therapist, teachers, everybody. And everybody has to have the same goal. Which for LaDainian for him to talk and be able to express himself. And to be back at his home school, for the second grade. I was just, so proud of our whole team. He also was starting his speech classes on December 30, 2016. And every Friday after that. So altogether he will have 3 days total out the week for speech.

DECEMBER 19, 2016

LaDainian goes to his grandma's house when he gets off the school bus almost every day. Over the weekend she had said she put up the Christmas tree. So, she did, and when he got over there she said he said oh oh-oh like Santa Clause do. She just started laughing. It's just all starting to come together. My research and my plans for him was really working. We were getting him back at his old school. if it took all we had in us and they had a Christmas party today in school.

So, he probably been hearing them say Merry Christmas all week in school. This was their last week of school this week.

DECEMBER 22, 2016

LaDainian birthday is today, and me and his dad took him out. We took him to the movies, and to Chuck E. Cheese by the end of the night he had gone to sleep in the car. My goal for him or plan for him over the Christmas break was to still do homework every night Monday to Friday and read to him every night. He was starting his speech classes on December 30, 2016. So we was going to have fun, work hard all at the same time. My goal for him and I said this many times in this book. My goal for him was to get him at his old school. And for him not to have to go to ESY during the summer break. And at our next IEP meeting we was going to talk about all that. Which like I said earlier was gonna be the spring time of 2017. So, it was our job to make sure he went to speech and do his homework every evening, every day while school was out during the Christmas break. He will not forget nothing he had learn up until this point in school, because the IEP meeting was coming up real soon. And he was still taking his vitamins, doing the juice, eating the muffins. You can't stop the routine just because school is out. You gotta keep going. That's the only way any of this will work. The more help they get the better.

JANUARY 4, 2017

LaDainian was still doing well. He was saying more and more words. He studied hard. My goal for him, I said this early in this book, is to get him to his old school and for him not to have to go to ESY during the summer break ESY-extended school year. At our next IEP meeting, we were going to talk about all that. That wasn't going to be until around the springtime. His teacher and his speech therapist were concerned about him forgetting some of the things he learned so far. Two weeks is a long time to be out of school, and they weren't going back to school until January 5, 2017. They were hoping he wouldn't forget all he had learned before the Christmas break. It was my job to make sure he went to speech class and do homework in the evening every day while school was out, just like in school, and he was still taking his vitamins, doing the muffins, and juice. You can't stop the routine just because school is out. The more help they get, the better.

JANUARY 5, 2017

LaDainian started going back to school today. The holiday break is over. We still did homework, and we had fun over the break, all at the same time. Our next IEP meeting was in the springtime 2017. That's when they will tell us if he needs ESY and what the plan for the next school year was. My plan or goal for him was for him not to need ESY and for him to go to his old school. I was going to do all I could for that goal to come true, and so far so good—he was doing great. ESY was for students who didn't do well in school and needs extra help during the summer break.

JANUARY 6, 2017

LaDainian had speech today at the speech clinic. He goes to speech first, and then to school. And he was crying when he was on his way to school. It's going to take time. It's an adjustment. But it's something that had to be done. He needed that extra help. Then he gotta adjust to going back to school after that long two weeks he was out of school for Christmas break. Yesterday was their first day back he will be OK.

JANUARY 9, 2017

LaDainian have more adjusting to do. We were getting ready to move again, and I was hoping he would be able to stay at the school he was at because he was doing so well, but at the same time, I was trying to make a better life for him, but that's life. Things are going to change. Your routine is going to change. You're going to get bumps and bruises, but you keep on going, and I think he will do okay. He probably will be looking like, why are we moving? Sometimes it takes him a minute to get used to things, but he will come around. He will get use to the move just like he had to get use to going to speech on Fridays before school. He doesn't cry any more going to school after speech. He used to cry every Friday going to school. But he got used to it. Hopefully he will not do too bad with all the changes.

JANUARY 11, 2017

LaDainian was surprising me every day. We had ordered pizza one night for dinner, and the pizza man knocked on the door. We open it, and LaDainian comes to the door and tells the pizza man, "Hello there!" He tells the Pizza Man this, "Hello there, man!" That was so funny, and he shook the man's hand, the channel becoming clearer every day. It's not all the way clear, but it's not all the way fuzzy no more. I knew it was a matter of time. It really does take a team—his parents, grandparents, teachers, speech therapist, and OT therapist. Your child's doctor, everybody has to be on the team. And everybody has to have the same goal. That goal for my son was getting him talking and on the same level as his peers. You need to have a plan to beat autism because it can be beaten. It will take some time, but it can be done. You just got to keep praying and keep faith that your child will pull through and never give up. That's what you got to do, and that's what I was doing, me and my team.

JANUARY 12, 2017

LaDainian loves Steve Harvey, and this was a while ago when he gets off the school bus, which was around 2:40 p.m. He likes to get off the bus and play, but at one time it seemed like I couldn't get a day off, so I was like we're going in the house. I wanted to watch *The Steve Harvey Show*, the talk show here in Smyrna, Georgia. It comes on at three. He was crying because I wanted to go in the house and he wanted to play. I came in the house. I put the TV on the channel Steve comes on, and next thing I knew, he stopped crying and started smiling and running around the house, laughing. So I asked his grandma, "When Boo goes over to your house after school, do y'all watch Steve Harvey?" And she said no. I said, "Man, this boy like to lose his mind." She was like, "What!" So ever since then we watched the Steve Harvey talk show "Little Big Shots" and "Family Feud" and turn from those shows if you want to and it's going to be war. He used to just say Steve. Now he say Steve Harvey his whole name, and I said I hope one day he can meet Steve Harvey. Maybe we can be on the Steve Harvey talk show. The only way my TV is not on Steve Harvey is if he is not on and he'd be saying those words on Family Feud.

JANUARY 15, 2017

Me and LaDainian's dad had found out that LaDainian was going to have to go to a new school starting February 1. We were moving, so he couldn't stay at the school he was at. I had just hoped and prayed that he would do well with all this adjusting he was doing between moving and going to speech therapy before school on Fridays. I just hope that he wouldn't feel overwhelmed but moving to a different place was best for him and all of us. He was about to go to a new school with a new teacher and new students. I mean he had done well when he went to ESY that one summer to a new school and new teacher, but kids that have autism don't like change. It's hard for them to adjust sometimes. I just hope that he would do well and his new teachers would treat him good.

JANUARY 20, 2017

LaDainian went to speech therapy last Friday, and the speech therapist was showing him flash cards with animals on them. It was a chicken on the first card, and she said "LaDainian, what is this?" And LaDainian said, "Chicken nuggets." He was supposed to name what animal was on the flash cards. His therapist said, "It's just a chicken." He said, "Chicken nuggets." He loves chicken nuggets. He was surprising us more each day, and when we told his teacher that same day when he got to the school she said, "Yeah he told us the same thing when we showed him a chicken. I just shook my head. I took him to the dentist on January 18, and all this time he never let them do x-rays, but this time he did, and all the nurses clapped for him. He had done real good. The first time he went he was so nervous he boo booed on himself. He has come a long way from that. He would get real nervous, but I had stopped taking him for a while, because he would just get so nervous. But they said no don't do that. The more he comes, the better he will do. I just hate to see him like that, being that nervous, that was scary to me, but now he's so much better.

JANUARY 28, 2017

LaDainian still cried when we dropped him off at school on Friday. He was still trying to adjust to going to speech class and then going to school. These days remind me of when he was in day care and he would cry every time he got dropped off, so I was praying with this new school that he was about to go to he would do great because it really was the best move for all of us. We couldn't stay here. He was talking more at this time, but he was going to have to change schools, and kids with Autism have a hard time with change. They like things to stay the same. The only thing that was staying the same was the speech therapy classes on Fridays at the same location.

FEBRUARY 5, 2017

LaDainian didn't cry much last Friday after he left speech class. He was having a hard time in the beginning trying to adjust to going to speech therapy and then to school, so he was doing better and talking more. He was doing so good at the speech clinic. He was making me so happy. He was improving.

FEBRUARY 7, 2017

LaDainian's grandma had asked him, "LaDainian, you realize you have moved?" He goes to his grandma's house all the time, so he was used to coming over here almost every day after school. I just had hoped and prayed he did well. He was about to have a new teacher at this new school he was about to go to. Sometimes it takes him awhile to get used to change, but he seemed to be okay at his new home. When he went to speech class last week, he didn't cry much when he got dropped off, not like he was the last couple of times, so he was adjusting going to speech class and then school, and he was doing so good in speech on Fridays. He had a doctor's appointment on February 6, 2017, and he did awesome. He let the doctor look at his ears, his mouth, everything. He did real good. I had to take him out for lunch. He had never done okay at the doctor's because he doesn't like going to the doctor's, but this time he did so good. He is getting older too. When he was a baby, he did good, but that was because he didn't know what was going on, but when he learned, we would have to hold him down so the doctor could check him out. I was so happy. This was his yearly checkup, so he was four feet three and a half inches tall and 52 lbs. He was only seven years old at this time. He is going to be real tall. I am a proud mom.

FEBRUARY 9, 2017

LaDainian did awesome in school yesterday for his first day at his new school. He did cry a little yesterday when he got dropped off, but his teacher said he cried only five minutes then he was over it. They said after it, he told them he wanted to eat, so they took him to the lunch room to get breakfast. They said he did so good. I was so happy to hear that news. I had been praying all day yesterday for him to have a great day in school, and he did. As a parent with a child with special needs you always hope and pray that you are doing the right thing for your child because you don't want your child to be uncomfortable or have any type of setbacks. I just hope and pray that I made the right choice in this move because we had to move from where we were, and then today he got dropped off and didn't even cry at all, so that made me feel better that he was doing good, and his teacher said it wasn't a requirement that they give out homework to the students. Now it might not be a requirement for the other students in his class, but it's a requirement for my son. She said, "If you want us to give you homework for him, then we can. You will return it to the school on Thursdays." So, I wrote her a note and told her yes he needed homework. I didn't want him to forget how to write his name and his ABCs, etc. I didn't want him to have a hard time in school like I did. Read more in my first book "The Truth You Didn't Know". He will be doing homework every day.

FEBRUARY 17, 2017

LaDainian was trying to adjust to going to school after speech therapy. Sometimes I think he was crying because he did not want to miss out on nothing. By this time we were going to speech over a month, and yeah, it takes him some time to adjust, but not this long, because he is good all the way until we get to the school and he doesn't even cry going to his new school no more, so I just think he is scared he is going to miss out on things. Overall, he is doing great with the new move and all.

MARCH 2, 2017

LaDainian's great grandma had called over the weekend from New York, and she said, "I can tell the difference in his speech over the phone." I said, "Yeah, he's doing great." She said, "The last time I was there he was still pulling you to the kitchen or wherever." I said, "Yeah, he was, but now he is telling you what he wants." She was so happy to hear that, that extra day in speech therapy was helping too. He was getting speech two days out of the week in school and one day outside of school.

MARCH 4, 2017

LaDainian was doing great with the new move and the new school his grandma took him to school last Friday after we got done with speech. I had to go to work, and she said he didn't cry or nothing when he got dropped off. She said he was all smiles. It really wasn't about him trying to adjust from going to speech and then to school. He just was crying because he didn't want to miss out on anything, scared he's going to miss something. That's just what I feel, but overall he was doing great at home and in school—thanks to prayer, his vitamins, his juice, and his muffins. Maybe one day, like I said earlier, I will write an updated book on LaDainian progress.

APRIL 2, 2017

LaDainian didn't like the juice I made for him. But what I did was I started him out with a very small cup. Like when you go to a restaurant, and you get some wings, and they give you that cup of dressing to dip your wings. That's the size I started him out with. And

I had to stand there until he drinks it all. And it came out to be real good. But he just didn't like it because it was not in the norm. I didn't care if we had to sit all night, he was gonna drink that juice. It takes a team. If I wasn't home, I was at work then his grandma would sit with him, and give him the juice.

MAY 25, 2017

LaDainian last day of school for the summer was yesterday. And he didn't need ESY this summer (Extended School Year) which was great. Because that was for students who had a hard time during the school year, and needed extra help. But that wasn't gonna stop us from having summer school at home. Just like we had done the summer before. Overall, he did great in 1st grade. I just didn't want him to forget anything he had learn during the school year. He did change schools during this school year, and some days he did have a hard time trying to adjust. Other then that he did great. Pray really do work. My plan for the summer break, was to get him out more, let him have the best summer ever. But at the same time, we still got work to do. Two months is a long time to be out of school. You could forget a lot during those two months. I was still doing his vitamins and his juice. That didn't stop just because school was out. He also still had speech every Friday at the speech clinic. And I was working on him getting another day at the speech clinic, so he would have two days at the speech clinic. This summer was a full summer. And for the juice. I didn't do the celery or the orange juice or the yams and for the muffins I just ended up doing banana, pear, apple, and cinnamon muffin. Because I didn't want the color of the muffins to change too much. I pealed the apple and pear first. If the color would have changed too much, he wouldn't want to eat them.

JUNE 10, 2017

LaDainian did not like that juice at all that I made for him. I had to almost pour it down his throat. But it was helping him to improve, so I could not stop. Just because he didn't like it. And the more I made the juice the better tasting it got. The taste wasn't the problem. He just didn't want it. I didn't care he was going to drink it. By this time, I had up the amount I was giving him. One day, I had given him some, and it was close to bedtime. And he could not sleep. Just kale and spinach by itself give you energy. I should have known better. But he was improving in his speech more and more. He was still going to speech during the summer break. That didn't stop also. LaDainian was doing great and we all were so happy and proud of him.

QUESTIONS YOU MAY HAVE:

1. What made you write a book about autism?

   I wanted to help other families out there and wanted families to read a book about autism from a regular person. I wanted people to read the research I did to help my son.

2. How do you see your son in the future?

   I see my son doing great! I see him in college playing sports, getting good grades, and someday having his own family.

3. What are your hopes for this book?

   My hopes for this book is that it will help other families out there, and they will do the research I did or start their own research. My goal and hope for this book was just to help whom I could.

4. Do you believe the research you did will help other families?

   Yes, I believe that it will help. It's helping my son. He has shown a lot of improvements. Maybe one day I will write an update on his progress because I don't ever plan on stopping giving him his vitamins, his juices, his muffins, or his PediaSure. My goal for him was to get him back at his home school. Meaning the school he started Pre-k at.

5. What type of kid is LaDainian?

LaDainian is a very loving kid who loves to give hugs, a very smart kid. Everybody who meets him just falls in love with him. People always stop us in the store saying how cute he is. He always has us laughing and on our toes. He always has a smile on his face.

6. Is your son still struggling with autism?

Well it's a process. It's not going away overnight. I wish he could go to bed one night and wake up and be cured, but the vitamins I give him are not medicine. It's vitamins, so it will take time, but he is doing great and making great progress. You just can never give up. I do believe the vitamins I'm giving him have helped him so much, and me getting him help early has also helped. The earlier, the better. That's the key, and he's been getting help since the age of three years old. I started getting help for him at 2 ½ years old and at 4 years old they told us he had Autism.

7. What do you want out of the new school year 2016–2017?

I hope and pray that he would do so good in school, that he could go back to his home school and learn all he could learn, do his very best and meet all his IEP goals for the school year, and go back to his home school for the 2nd grade. That was my hope and what I wanted for him for the new school year 2016–2017.

HOW I MADE LADAINIAN MUFFINS:

One box of cornbread mix (whatever your family like): 2 bananas, chopped 2 apples 2 pears 2 tablespoons honey 2 eggs 1/2 half cup milk (whatever kind your family drinks; my family drinks Lactaid milk)

What I did was mix the cornbread muffin, mix with the eggs, milk, and honey together. Then I put in my blender bananas, apples, and pears. I peeled the apples and pears. Blend all those together, but don't blend too much. Make sure it is kind of thick and smooth. You don't want it too thin. Make sure you spray your muffin pans with a spray oil (whatever kind you like). Heat oven on 400 F for fifteen to twenty minutes. I came up with these muffins because I wanted a plan B just in case the juice does not work out. My son loves muffins, as I said earlier. I had to come up with ways to get him to eat more than just nuggets and fries. Even if he liked the juice, I still wanted to try the muffins. That would be another treat for us on the weekends. We all were gonna try out these muffins, make sure the fruits and vegetables are fresh for the muffins and juice.

CAN'T WAIT

Can't wait for the day when I can ask my kids "What do you want to do today?" and I won't have to worry about how much it will cost. Can't wait for the day when money is not an issue. Can't wait for the day when my kids can run free in their own backyard. Can't wait until the day comes when I don't have to work at somebody else's job making them money. Can't wait until the day comes for my son to start talking and he is back at his old school. Can't wait when the day comes when I'm sitting on my back porch drinking sweet tea watching my kids play. Can't wait for the day when I am walking down the aisle in my white dress. Can't wait for the day to come and all my books are out helping families (*The Truth You Didn't Know* and *On the Road to Saying Bye to Autism*, just naming a few). I can't wait for the day where I can tell my kids I worked hard so you all have a great life. Can't wait for the day when I can look in my closet and ask myself, "What do I want to wear?" Can't wait for the day when I tell my son, "You are going to have a brother or sister." Can't wait for the day when we can travel and don't have to worry about coming back. Can't wait for the day when I'm worry-free from bills and work. Can't wait for the day when I can buy my kids a dog for a pet. Can't wait for the day when I can say autism is no more in my family and yours. I just can't wait.

—Lakisha Marie Mackie

"Taking pictures before school."

"First day of school 2022"

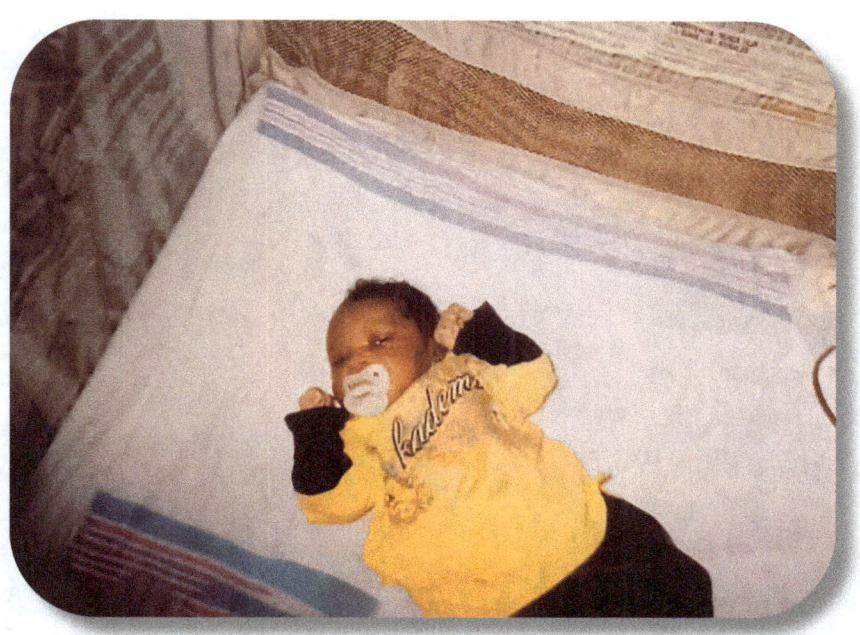

"At home in bed."

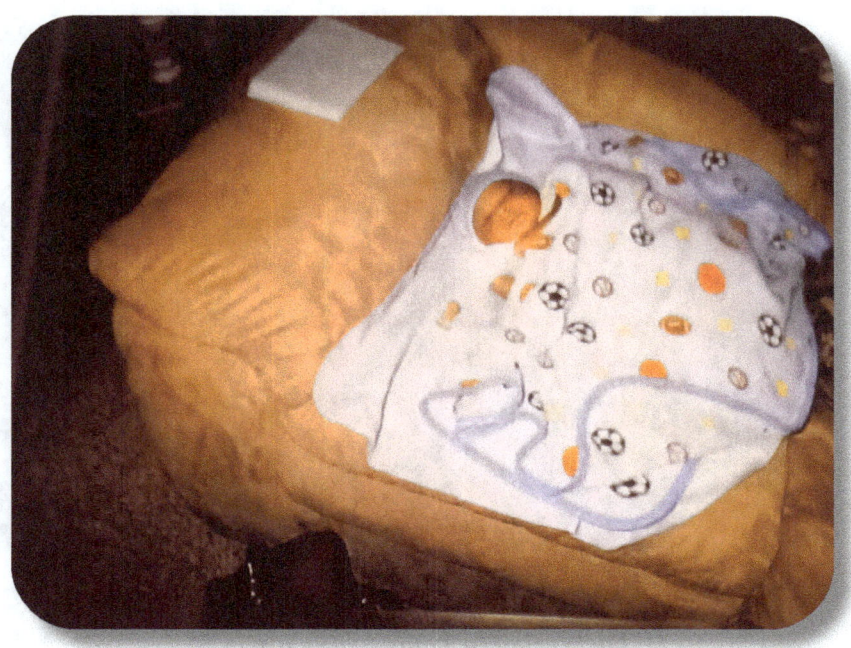

"Born on December 22, 2009 7lbs 15 ounces 21 1/2 inches long"

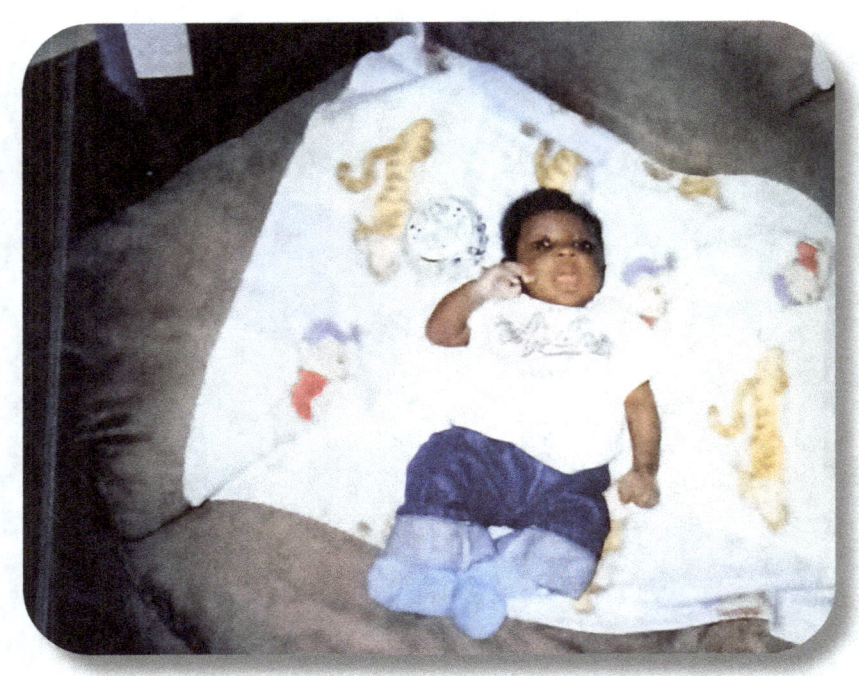

"LaDainian holding his balloon at 3 months old."

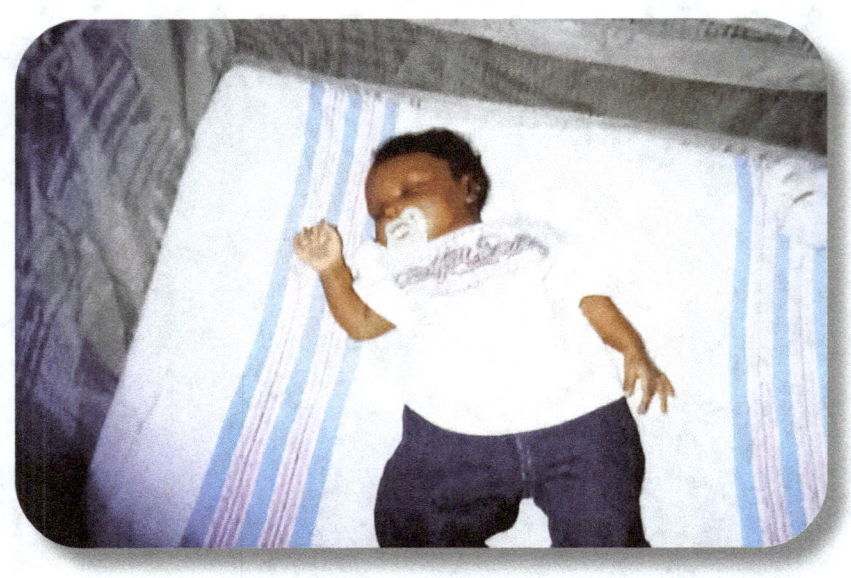

"LaDainian at home taking a nap."

"Getting ready for school."

"Out to eat celebrating our Anniversary 2009."

*"First book signing at J.R. Crickets South
Cobb Drive Smyrna Ga. 30080"*

"LaDainian standing in front of a car on his 12th birthday."

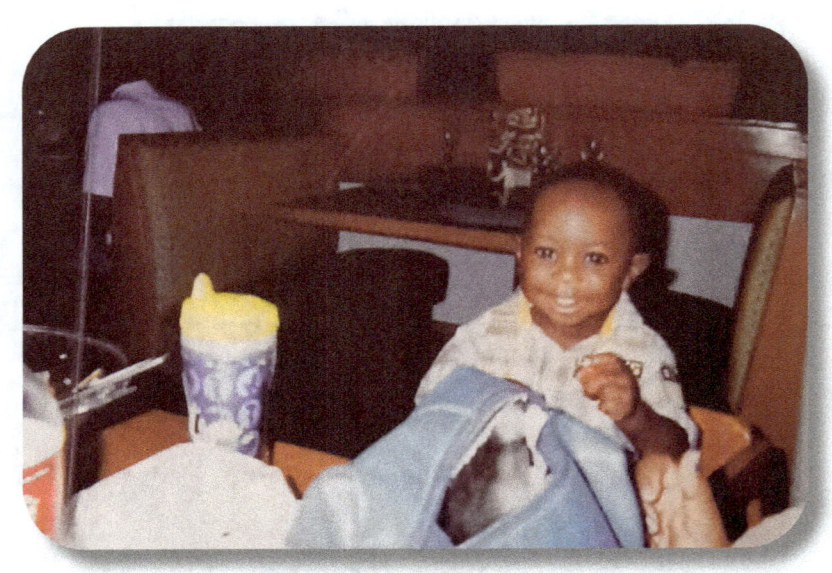

"LaDainian is out to eat!!"

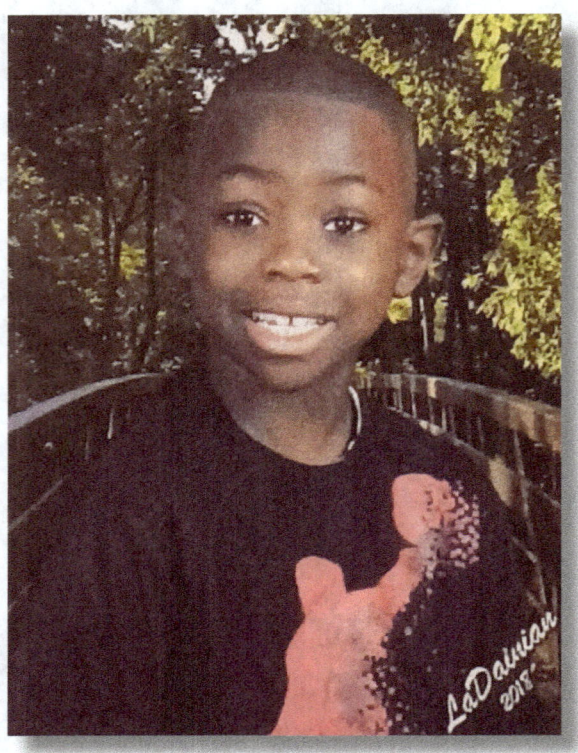

"2017-2018 School Year picture of LaDainian"

"Standing in the house by the front door."

"School picture day. 2022"

ZJ